Appendix

- Answer Key
- Scoring Guidelines for Open-Ended Questions
- Scoring Rubrics for Open-Ended Questions
- Vocabulary List
- Answer Sheet

Answer Key: Vocabulary

Practice 1 (p. 12)
1. D   2. A   3. C   4. C   5. B
6. C   7. C   8. D

Practice 2 (p. 13)
1. C   2. B   3. D   4. D   5. A
6. C   7. C   8. A

Practice 3 (p. 14)
1. C   2. A   3. B   4. D   5. D
6. B   7. C   8. D

Practice 4 (p. 15)
1. D   2. D   3. C   4. A   5. B
6. D   7. D   8. C

Practice 5 (p. 16)
1. C   2. B   3. D   4. D   5. B
6. A   7. C   8. D

Practice 6 (p. 17)
1. D   2. A   3. B   4. C   5. C
6. D   7. D   8. B

Practice 7 (p. 18)
1. C   2. D   3. A   4. D   5. B
6. C   7. D   8. B

Practice 8 (p. 19)
1. B   2. C   3. C   4. D   5. B
6. A   7. D   8. C

Practice 9 (p. 20)
1. B   2. A   3. D   4. C   5. A
6. D   7. B   8. C

Practice 10 (p. 21)
1. C   2. D   3. A   4. A   5. C
6. B   7. A   8. D

Practice 11 (p. 22)
1. C   2. B   3. D   4. C   5. A
6. D   7. B   8. C

Practice 12 (p. 23)
1. D   2. C   3. D   4. B   5. C
6. B   7. A   8. D

Practice 13 (p. 24)
1. C   2. D   3. B   4. C   5. C
6. A   7. D   8. C   9. B   10. C

Practice 14 (p. 25)
1. D   2. A   3. C   4. C   5. D
6. B   7. D   8. C   9. D   10. D

Practice 15 (p. 26)
1. A   2. C   3. C   4. B   5. D
6. C   7. D   8. D   9. B   10. C

Practice 16 (p. 27)
1. D   2. C   3. D   4. C   5. A
6. C   7. D   8. C   9. B   10. D

Practice 17 (p. 28)
1. C   2. B   3. D   4. D   5. B
6. C   7. A   8. D

Practice 18 (p. 29)
1. B   2. D   3. C   4. C   5. D
6. B   7. C   8. D

Practice 19 (p. 30)
1. B   2. D   3. D   4. C   5. C
6. B   7. A   8. D

Answer Key: Comprehension

1: Do you know how to to make recycled paper? (p. 32)

1. C	2. D	3. A	4. D	5. C
6. C	7. B	8. B	9. C	10. B
11. C	12. D	13. A	14. B	15. C
16. D	17. B	18. B	19. See scoring

guidelines and rubrics

2: It's a Noisy World Out There! (p. 37)

1. C	2. C	3. A	4. D	5. D
6. B	7. B	8. C	9. D	10. A
11. D	12. C	13. D	14. C	15. A
16. C	17. D	18. & 19. See scoring

guidelines and rubrics

3: Two Poems (p. 43)

1. B	2. C	3. D	4. C	5. B
6. B	7. D	8. C	9. D	

10. & 11. See scoring guidelines and rubrics

4: Athena and Arachne (p. 47)

1. C	2. A	3. C	4. D	5. C
6. D	7. C	8. B	9. B	10. A
11. C	12. C	13. B	14. C	15. D
16. A	17. See scoring guidelines and rubrics

5: Along Came a Spider (p. 52)

1. D	2. A	3. C	4. C	5. C
6. D	7. A	8. D	9. A	10. C
11. B	12. D	13. A	14. D	15. C
16. C	17. See scoring guidelines and rubrics

6: A Simple Way to Save Lives (p. 56)

1. D	2. B	3. C	4. C	5. D
6. B	7. C	8. C	9. C	10. A
11. B	12. C	13. D	14. C	15. C
16. A	17. D	18. & 19. See scoring

guidelines and rubrics

7: The Wind in a Frolic (p. 62)

1. C	2. D	3. A	4. B	5. D
6. B	7. A	8. D	9. B	10. C
11. D	12. & 13. See scoring guidelines and

rubrics

8: A Tree from the Past (p. 67)

1. C	2. B	3. D	4. A	5. D
6. C	7. C	8. D	9. B	10. B
11. A	12. B	13. B	14. C	15. B
16. C	17. D	18. D	19. C	

20a. & 20b. See scoring guidelines and rubrics

9: Follow the Bouncing Ball (p. 74)

1. B	2. D	3. D	4. C	5. C
6. A	7. C	8. D	9. A	10. C
11. A	12. C	13. D		

14. & 15. See scoring guidelines and rubrics

10: How People Learned to Measure and Count (p. 80)

1. C	2. C	3. D	4. B	5. D
6. B	7. A	8. C	9. C	10. D
11. C	12. D	13. B		

14. & 15. See scoring guidelines and rubrics

11: What kind of shopper are you? (p. 85)

1. D	2. C	3. B	4. D	5. C
6. C	7. A	8. B	9. D	10. C
11. C	12. B	13. D	14. D	15. C

16. See scoring guidelines and rubrics

12: The Elephant That Will Not Move (p. 90)

1. C	2. B	3. D	4. C	5. D
6. A	7. C	8. D	9. C	10. B
11. D	12. C	13. B	14. B	15. C

16. See scoring guidelines and rubrics

13: Into the Primitive (p. 94)

1. D	2. B	3. D	4. C	5. D
6. D	7. C	8. B	9. B	10. B
11. C	12. C	13. B	14. D	15. C
16. B	17. D	18. C	19. C	

20. See scoring guidelines and rubrics

Answer Key: Study Skills

Practice 1 (p. 100)
1. D 2. B 3. D 4. A 5. C
6. C 7. C 8. C

Practice 2 (p. 101)
1. C 2. C 3. B 4. D 5. C

Practice 3 (pp. 102–103)
1. C 2. B 3. C 4. C 5. B
6. B 7. B 8. C 9. D

Practice 4 (pp. 104–105)
1. D 2. A 3. C 4. D 5. B
6. D 7. C

Practice 5 (pp. 106–107)
1. C 2. B 3. D 4. C 5. D
6. B 7. C 8. B 9. A

Practice 6 (p. 108)
1. D 2. B 3. C 4. B 5. D
6. A

Practice 7 (p. 109)
1. C 2. C 3. B 4. A 5. B
6. D 7. D 8. D

Practice 8 (p. 110)
1. C 2. B 3. A 4. D 5. C
6. C 7. A 8. D 9. B 10. D

Practice 9 (p. 111)
1. C 2. D 3. C 4. D

Practice 10 (pp. 112–113)
1. C 2. B 3. A 4. D 5. B
6. B 7. D 8. A 9. D

Practice 11 (pp. 114–115)
1. D 2. C 3. C 4. B 5. B
6. C 7. D 8. A 9. A 10. B

Practice 12 (p. 116)
1. D 2. C 3. D 4. D 5. C

TestSMART®

for Reading Skills and Comprehension—Grade 8
Aligned to State and National Standards

Help for

Basic Reading Skills

State Competency Tests

Achievement Tests

by

Lori Mammen

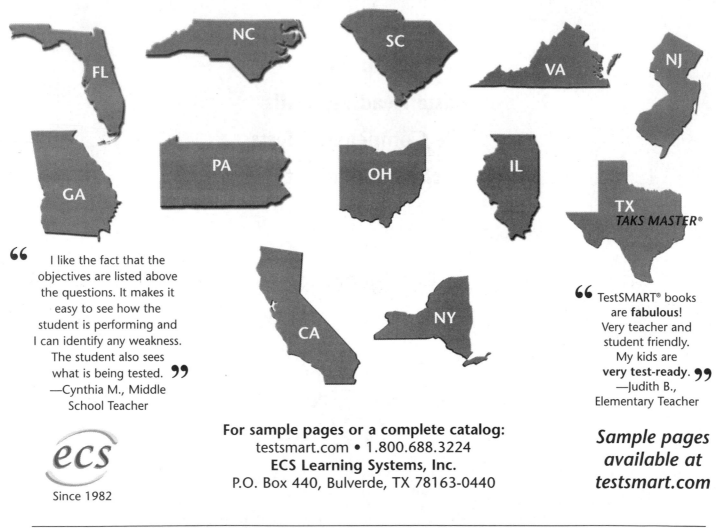

Book Cover: Kirstin Simpson **Book Design:** Educational Media Services

---

Contents

Welcome to *TestSMART* ®!!

It's just the tool you need
to help students review important reading skills and
prepare for standardized reading tests!

Introduction

During the past several years, an increasing number of American students have faced some form of state-mandated competency testing in reading. While several states use established achievement tests, such as the Iowa Test of Basic Skills (ITBS), to assess students' reading ability, other states' reading assessments focus on the skills and knowledge emphasized in their particular reading curriculum. Texas, for example, has administered a state-developed assessment since 1980. The New York State Testing Program began in 1999 and tests both fourth- and eighth-grade students in reading.

Whatever the testing route, one point is very clear: the trend toward more and more competency testing is widespread and intense. By the spring of 1999, 48 states had adopted some type of reading assessment for students at various grade levels. In some states, these tests are "high-stakes" events that determine whether a student is promoted to the next grade level in school.

The emphasis on competency tests has grown directly from the national push for higher educational standards and accountability. Under increasing pressure from political leaders, business people, and the general public, policy-makers have turned to testing as a primary way to measure and improve student performance.

Although experienced educators know that such test results can reveal only a small part of a much broader educational picture, state-mandated competency tests have gained a strong foothold. Teachers must find effective ways to help their students prepare for these tests—and this is where *TestSMART* ® plays an important role.

What's inside this book?

Designed to help students review and practice important reading and test-taking skills, *TestSMART* ® includes reproducible practice exercises in the following areas—

- vocabulary
- comprehension
- study skills

In addition, each *TestSMART* ® book includes—

- a master skills list based on reading standards of several states
- a comprehensive vocabulary list
- complete answer keys for multiple-choice questions
- scoring guidelines and rubrics for open-ended questions
- a reproducible answer sheet

4

The content of each section of *TestSMART®* is outlined below.

Vocabulary: This section of *TestSMART®* includes 19 practice exercises with questions that focus on—

- demonstrating knowledge of root words and structural cues (Practices 1–4)
- using context clues to determine word meaning (Practices 5–9)
- recognizing the correct meaning of a word with multiple meanings (Practices 10–12)
- demonstrating knowledge of synonyms and antonyms (Practices 13–16)
- demonstrating knowledge of word analogies (Practices 17–19)

(Note: Vocabulary skills addressed in this section are also addressed in the reading comprehension section of TestSMART®.)

Comprehension: This section of *TestSMART®* includes—

- 13 reading passages, which include nonfiction, fiction, and poetry selections
- multiple-choice and open-ended questions for each passage
- tag-lines that identify the skill(s) addressed in each question

Reading skills addressed in this section include—

- determining the meaning of words *(root words, context clues, multiple-meaning words, synonyms/antonyms)*
- identifying supporting ideas *(facts/details, sequential order, written directions, setting)*
- summarizing written texts *(main idea, summary of major ideas/themes/ procedures)*

- perceiving relationships and recognizing outcomes *(cause/effect, predictions, similarities/differences)*
- analyzing information to make inferences and generalizations *(inferences, interpretations/ conclusions, generalizations, character analysis)*
- recognizing points of view, propaganda, and statements of fact/opinion *(fact/opinion, author's purpose)*
- reading, analyzing, and interpreting literature *(genre identification, genre characteristics, literary elements, figurative language)*

Study Skills: This section of *TestSMART®* includes 12 practice exercises that focus on identifying and using sources of different types of information (graphic sources, parts of a book, dictionary skills). Specific skills addressed in this section include—

- using parts of a book (Practice 1)
- interpreting charts, diagrams, and graphs (Practices 4 and 9)
- using a library card catalog (Practice 5)
- interpreting practical reading material (Practices 2–3, 6, and 10)
- recognizing and using dictionary skills (Practice 7)
- identifying appropriate sources of information (Practices 7–8 and 10)
- interpreting maps (Practices 11–12)

5

Master Skills List/Correlation Chart:
The reading skills addressed in
TestSMART® are based on the reading
standards and/or test specifications from
several different states. No two states have
identical wordings for their skills lists,
but there are strong similarities from one
state's list to another. Of course, the skills
needed for effective reading do not change
from one place to another. The Master
Skills List for Reading (page 9) represents
a synthesis of the reading skills
emphasized in various states. Teachers
who use this book will recognize the skills
that are stressed, even though the wording
of a few objectives may vary slightly from
that found in their own state's test
specifications. The Master Skills
Correlation Chart (page 10) offers a place
to identify the skills common to both
TestSMART® and a specific state
competency test.

Vocabulary List: A list of vocabulary
words appears on page 126. This list
includes many of the words tested in the
vocabulary section of this book and in
questions that accompany some of the
passages. Teachers and students can use
this list to create—

* word games
* word walls
* writing activities
* "word-of-the-day" activities
* synonym/antonym charts
* word webs
* analogies
* … and more

A word of caution: In general, teachers
should not ask students to memorize the
words and their meanings. While some
tests ask students to simply "know" the
meaning of selected vocabulary words,
the majority of tests emphasize using
structural cues and context clues to
determine the meaning of unfamiliar
words encountered during reading.

Answer Keys: Complete answer keys for
multiple-choice questions appear on pages
118–120.

Scoring Guidelines and Rubrics: The
scoring guidelines and sample rubrics
on pages 121–125 provide important
information for evaluating responses to
open-ended questions. (*Note: If a
state's assessment does not include open-
ended questions, teachers may use the
open-ended items in TestSMART® as
appropriate for their students.*) The
scoring guidelines indicate the expected
contents of successful responses. For
example, if an open-ended question asks
students to create a new title for a passage
and give reasons for their answer, the
scoring guideline for that question
suggests specific points that students
should include in the answer.

The sample rubrics allow teachers to
rate the overall effectiveness and
thoroughness of an answer. Once again,
consider the example of creating a new
title for a passage and supporting the
answer with specific reasons. The
corresponding rubric for that question
indicates the number and quality of the
reasons necessary to earn a score of "4"
(for an effective, complete response) or
a score of "1" (for an ineffective,
incomplete response).

6

How to Use This Book

Effective Test Preparation: What is the most effective way to prepare students for any reading competency test? Experienced educators know that the best test preparation includes three critical components—

- a strong curriculum that includes the content and skills to be tested
- effective and varied instructional methods that allow students to learn content and skills in many different ways
- targeted practice that familiarizes students with the specific content and format of the test they will take

Obviously, a strong curriculum and effective, varied instructional methods provide the foundation for all appropriate test preparation. Contrary to what some might believe, merely "teaching the test" performs a great disservice to students. Students must acquire knowledge, practice skills, and have specific educational experiences which can never be included on tests limited by time and in scope. For this reason, books like *TestSMART®* should **never** become the heart of the curriculum or a replacement for strong instructional methods.

Targeted Practice: *TestSMART®* does, however, address the final element of effective test preparation (targeted test practice) in the following ways—

- *TestSMART®* familiarizes students with the content usually included in competency tests.
- *TestSMART®* familiarizes students with the general format of such tests.

When students become familiar with both the content and the format of a test, they know what to expect on the actual test. This, in turn, improves their chances for success.

Using *TestSMART®*: Used as part of the regular curriculum, *TestSMART®* allows teachers to—

- pretest skills needed for the actual test students will take
- determine students' areas of strength and/or weakness
- provide meaningful test-taking practice for students
- ease students' test anxiety
- communicate test expectations and content to parents

Other Suggestions for Instruction: *TestSMART®* can serve as a springboard for other effective instructional activities that help with test preparation.

Group Work: Teacher and students work through selected practice exercises together, noting the kinds of questions and the range of answer choices. They discuss common errors for each kind of question and strategies for avoiding these errors.

Predicting Answers: Students predict the correct answer before reading the given answer choices. This encourages students to think through the question rather than focus on finding the right answer. Students then read the given answer choices and determine which one, if any, matches the answer they have given.

Developing Test Questions: Once students become familiar with the format of test questions, they develop "test-type" questions for other assigned reading (e.g., science, social studies).

Vocabulary Development: Teacher and students foster vocabulary development in all subject areas through the use of word walls, word webs, word games, synonym/antonym charts, analogies, word categories, "word-of-the-day" activities, etc.

Two-Sentence Recaps: Students regularly summarize what they have read in one or two sentences. For fiction,

students use the basic elements (setting, characters, problem, solution) to guide their summaries. For nonfiction, students use the journalist's questions (who, what, where, when, why) for the same purpose. The teacher may also list 3–5 key words from a reading selection and direct students to write a one- to two-sentence summary that includes the given words.

Generalizations: After students read a selection, the teacher states a generalization based on the reading, and students provide specific facts and details to support the generalization; or the teacher provides specifics from the selection, and students state the generalization.

8

Master Skills List

I.   Determine the meaning of words in written texts
A. Use root words and other structural cues to recognize new words
B. Use context clues to determine word meaning
C. Recognize correct meaning of words with multiple meanings
D. Demonstrate knowledge of synonyms, antonyms, and homophones
E. Choose the correct word to complete an analogy

II.   Identify supporting ideas
A. Identify relevant facts and details
B. Use text structure (e.g., headings, subheadings) to locate relevant facts and details
C. Sequence events in chronological order (e.g., story events, steps in process)
D. Follow written directions

III.   Summarize a variety of written texts
A. Determine the main idea or essential message of a text
B. Paraphrase or summarize the major ideas, themes, or procedures of a text

IV.   Perceive relationships and recognize outcomes
A. Identify cause and effect relationships in a text
B. Make and verify predictions with information from a text
C. Connect, compare, and contrast ideas, themes, and issues across texts
D. Respond to texts by making observations/connections, speculating, questioning, etc.

V.   Analyze information in order to make inferences and generalizations
A. Make and explain inferences (e.g., main idea, conclusion, moral, cause/effect)
B. Support interpretations/conclusions with information from text(s)
C. Make generalizations based on information from a text

VI.   Recognize points of view, propaganda, and statements of fact and opinion
A. Distinguish fact from opinion in a text
B. Identify the author's purpose
C. Recognize logical, ethical, and emotional appeals
D. Analyze positions, arguments, and evidence presented by an author
E. Identify bias and propaganda

VII.   Read, analyze, and interpret literature
A. Identify genres of fiction, nonfiction, and poetry
B. Identify characteristics representative of a given genre
C. Identify important literary elements (e.g., theme, setting, plot, character, conflict)
D. Recognize/interpret figurative language (e.g., simile, metaphor, hyperbole, idiom, allusion)
E. Recognize use of sound devices (e.g., rhyme, alliteration, onomatopoeia)

VIII.   Identify and use sources of different types of information
A. Use and interpret graphic sources of information (e.g., charts, graphs)
B. Use reference resources and the parts of a book (e.g., index) to locate information
C. Recognize and use dictionary skills

Master Skills Correlation Chart

Use this chart to identify the skills included on a specific state competency test. To correlate the skills to a specific state's objectives, find and mark those skills common to both. The first column shows a sample correlation based on the Texas Assessment of Knowledge and Skills (TAKS).

		Sample Correlation	
I.	**Determine the meaning of words in written texts**		
	A. Use root words and other structural cues to recognize new words	*	
	B. Use context clues to determine word meaning	*	
	C. Recognize correct meaning of words with multiple meanings	*	
	D. Demonstrate knowledge of synonyms, antonyms, and homophones		
	E. Choose the correct word to complete an analogy		
II.	**Identify supporting ideas**		
	A. Identify relevant facts and details	*	
	B. Use text structure (e.g., headings, subheadings) to locate relevant facts and details	*	
	C. Sequence events in chronological order	*	
	D. Follow written directions		
III.	**Summarize a variety of written texts**		
	A. Determine the main idea or essential message of a text	*	
	B. Summarize the major ideas, themes, or procedures of a text	*	
IV.	**Perceive relationships and recognize outcomes**		
	A. Identify cause and effect relationships	*	
	B. Make and verify predictions with information from text	*	
	C. Connect, compare, and contrast ideas, themes, and issues across texts	*	
	D. Respond to texts by making observations/connections, speculating, questioning		
V.	**Analyze information in order to make inferences and generalizations**		
	A. Make and explain inferences	*	
	B. Support interpretations/conclusions with information from a text	*	
	C. Make generalizations based on information from a text	*	
VI.	**Recognize points of view, propaganda, and statements of fact and opinion**		
	A. Distinguish fact from opinion	*	
	B. Identify the author's purpose	*	
	C. Recognize logical, ethical, and emotional appeals	*	
	D. Analyze positions, arguments, and evidence presented by an author	*	
	E. Identify bias and propaganda	*	
VII.	**Read, analyze, and interpret literature**		
	A. Identify genres of fiction, nonfiction, and poetry		
	B. Identify characteristics representative of a given genre		
	C. Identify important literary elements	*	
	D. Recognize/interpret figurative language		
	E. Recognize use of sound devices		
VIII.	**Identify and use sources of different types of information**		
	A. Use and interpret graphic sources of information	*	
	B. Use reference resources and the parts of a book to locate information		
	C. Recognize and use dictionary skills		

Vocabulary

I. Determine the meaning of words in written texts

    A. Use root words and other structural cues to recognize new words
    B. Use context clues to determine word meaning
    C. Recognize correct meaning of words with multiple meanings
    D. Demonstrate knowledge of synonyms and antonyms
    E. Choose the correct word to complete an analogy

11

Practice 1: Root Words and Structural Cues

Directions: Read each question. On your answer sheet, darken the circle for each correct response.

1. Which word probably comes from the Latin word *erumpere*, which means "to break"?

   A era

   B errand

   C error

   D erupt

2. The word **exile** probably comes from the Latin word—

   A *exsul*, meaning wanderer

   B *exemplum*, meaning example

   C *excepere*, meaning to pick out

   D *exigere*, meaning to weigh out

3. Which word probably comes from the Latin word *facere*, meaning "to make"?

   A facial

   B faculty

   C factory

   D faking

4. In the words **enshrine** and **entangle**, the prefix **en** means—

   A before

   B under

   C in

   D above

5. In the words **displease** and **disrespect** the prefix **dis** means—

   A within

   B the absence of

   C beneath

   D over or above

6. The word **reflection** comes from the Latin word *reflectere*, meaning "to bend back." Which word is most closely related in meaning to the word **reflection**?

   A recover

   B refresh

   C reflex

   D reform

7. Which word probably comes from the Latin word *procedere*, meaning "to advance"?

   A problem

   B production

   C procession

   D protest

8. In the words **delegation** and **interruption**, the suffix **tion** indicates that both words are—

   A adjectives

   B adverbs

   C verbs

   D nouns

I.A *Use root words and other structural cues to recognize new words*

Practice 2: Roots Words and Structural Cues

Directions: Read each question. On your answer sheet, darken the circle for each correct response.

1. Which word probably comes from the Latin word *tempus*, which means "time"?

   A tender

   B temper

   C tempo

   D tempt

2. Which word probably comes from the Latin word *spirare*, which means "to breathe"?

   A instant

   B inspire

   C inspect

   D insist

3. Which word probably comes from the Greek word *arkhein*, meaning "to rule"?

   A action

   B arch

   C monster

   D monarch

4. In the words **socialize** and **symbolize**, the suffix **ize** means—

   A tend to

   B cross

   C connect

   D make

5. The word **minute** probably comes from the Latin word—

   A *minutus*, meaning small

   B *moneta*, meaning money

   C *usare*, meaning to use

   D *ultra*, meaning beyond

6. Which word probably comes from the Latin word *sanus*, meaning "healthy"?

   A sandal

   B sandy

   C sane

   D sassy

7. In the words **transmit** and **transplant**, the prefix **trans** means—

   A around

   B after

   C across

   D above

8. In the words **attentive** and **sensitive**, the suffix **ive** indicates that both words are—

   A adjectives

   B adverbs

   C nouns

   D verbs

I.A   Use root words and other structural cues to recognize new words

13

Practice 3. Root Words and Structural Cues

Directions: Read each question. On your answer sheet, darken the circle for each correct response.

1. Which word probably comes from the Latin word *devovere*, which means "to promise"?

   A defend

   B device

   C devotion

   D develop

2. Which word probably comes from the Latin word *discors*, which means "disagreeing"?

   A discord

   B distant

   C discount

   D dispatch

3. Which word probably comes from the Greek word *aristos*, meaning "best"?

   A arid

   B aristocrat

   C artistic

   D astronomy

4. In the words **imperfect** and **improper**, the prefix **im** means—

   A into

   B beneath

   C between

   D not

5. The word **sequence** probably comes from the Latin word—

   A *secare*, meaning to cut

   B *severus*, meaning serious

   C *servus*, meaning slave

   D *sequi*, meaning to follow

6. Which word probably comes from the Latin word *ventus*, meaning "wind"?

   A velvet

   B ventilate

   C verse

   D vessel

7. In the words **foreseen** and **foretell**, the prefix **fore** means—

   A away from

   B among

   C ahead

   D between

8. In the words **available** and **preferable**, the suffix **able** indicates that both words are—

   A verbs

   B nouns

   C adverbs

   D adjectives

I.A Use root words and other structural cues to recognize new words

Practice 4: Root Words and Structural Cues

Directions: Read each question. On your answer sheet, darken the circle for each correct response.

1. Which word probably does NOT come from the Greek word *monos*, which means "one"?

   A monopoly

   B monocle

   C monarch

   D monster

2. Which word probably comes from the Latin word *docere*, which means "to teach"?

   A decide

   B dock

   C document

   D docile

3. Which word probably does NOT come from the Latin word *flectere*, meaning "to bend"?

   A reflect

   B reflex

   C flicker

   D flexible

4. In the words **interact** and **intertwine**, the prefix **inter** means—

   A between

   B within

   C into

   D beneath

5. The word **evacuate** probably comes from the Latin word—

   A *vadare*, meaning to go

   B *vacare*, meaning to be empty

   C *vacca*, meaning cow

   D *vagus*, meaning wandering

6. Which word probably comes from the Greek *khronikos*, which means "of time"?

   A nocturnal

   B knowledgeable

   C crystallize

   D chronicle

7. In the words **expelled** and **extract**, the prefix **ex** means—

   A within

   B among

   C into

   D out

8. In the words **intramural** and **intravenous**, the prefix **intra** means—

   A between

   B without

   C within

   D beyond

I.A Use root words and other structural cues to recognize new words

15

Practice 5: Context Clues

Directions: Read the following sentences. Then choose the best word to fit in the blank. On your answer sheet, darken the circle for the correct answer.

1. My favorite artists are those who do an excellent job at _____ scenes from nature.
   A dictating
   B discharging
   C depicting
   D duplicating

2. My father relies on his business _____ whenever he must negotiate a deal.
   A expectation
   B expertise
   C exposure
   D example

3. The audience thoroughly enjoyed the comedian's _____ routine.
   A favorable
   B elaborate
   C knowledgeable
   D hilarious

4. The Animal Defense League encourages the _____ treatment of animals.
   A marginal
   B lapsed
   C frustrating
   D humane

5. The explorers discovered the old pirate ship _____ in water.
   A propelled
   B submerged
   C relapsed
   D wrenched

6. My grandmother often quotes a _____ to prove her point.
   A proverb
   B suspicion
   C passion
   D renewal

7. Participating in the class play was _____ and did not affect a student's grade in the class.
   A multiple
   B standard
   C optional
   D symbolic

8. Given a choice between eating spinach or eating ice cream, most children will choose the _____ .
   A surplus
   B merit
   C motive
   D latter

I.B   Use context clues to determine word meaning

Practice 6: Context Clues

Directions: Read the following sentences. Then choose the best word to fit in the blank. On your answer sheet, darken the circle for the correct answer.

1. The doctor performed surgery to remove the _____ in the boy's throat.

   A separation

   B annoyance

   C friction

   D obstruction

2. The gracious hostess gave everyone a _____ greeting.

   A cordial

   B harsh

   C defective

   D favorable

3. During the early days of film, many people enjoyed the _____ adventures of the Three Stooges.

   A shimmering

   B madcap

   C ferocious

   D aggressive

4. With the right amount of water and sunlight, the plants should _____ in your garden.

   A billow

   B ignite

   C flourish

   D fortify

5. Of the five people interviewed by the manager, Toni was clearly the most qualified _____ .

   A respondent

   B delegate

   C applicant

   D presenter

6. Onions and garlic certainly have _____ odors.

   A crucial

   B imperfect

   C excess

   D distinctive

7. Beth and Jason are both excellent students and make _____ grades in school.

   A selective

   B stationary

   C duplicate

   D comparable

8. The architect can _____ a new shopping mall where the old factory now stands.

   A identify

   B envision

   C constrain

   D transform

I.B   Use context clues to determine word meaning

Practice 7: Context Clues

Directions: Read the following sentences. Then choose the best word to fit in the blank. On your answer sheet, darken the circle for the correct answer.

1. During the summer, people in the South must _____ both extreme heat and high humidity.

   A exceed

   B grudge

   C endure

   D condense

2. My grandfather asked me to _____ a plan for keeping insects out of his garden.

   A inflate

   B overcome

   C transmit

   D devise

3. Sometimes it is difficult to _____ the actual worth of old jewelry.

   A appraise

   B distribute

   C impair

   D specialize

4. The flowers were primarily yellow, with just a _____ of orange.

   A merit

   B kernel

   C token

   D tinge

5. The contestant showed true _____ when she won the contest.

   A premium

   B elation

   C convenience

   D acceptance

6. The teacher encouraged the children to _____ during the party.

   A rouse

   B overrule

   C interact

   D bicker

7. The couple planned a simple ceremony without _____ decorations or refreshments.

   A available

   B casual

   C evident

   D elaborate

8. Mr. Chacko returned the _____ tire and requested a replacement.

   A respectable

   B defective

   C flexible

   D invalid

I.B   Use context clues to determine word meaning

Practice 8: Context Clues

Directions: Read the following sentences. Then choose the best word to fit in the blank. On your answer sheet, darken the circle for the correct answer.

1. When the motor failed, the boys used oars to _____ the boat.
   A puncture
   B propel
   C outpace
   D resolve

2. The florist advised us to be more _____ when we choose flowers for the stage.
   A stationary
   B tolerant
   C selective
   D available

3. Unlike dogs and cats, tigers are not _____ animals.
   A hardy
   B elegant
   C domestic
   D preferable

4. Nisha did not hear us because she was _____ with her homework.
   A literary
   B territorial
   C significant
   D preoccupied

5. Before ordering the carpet, Mrs. Tran needed to know the _____ of her living room.
   A inflections
   B dimensions
   C requirements
   D standards

6. During the party, I enjoyed _____ with the other guests.
   A mingling
   B lingering
   C confining
   D entrusting

7. Jarod _____ the note and tossed it on the floor.
   A exceeded
   B dispatched
   C cringed
   D crumpled

8. My mother often _____ me for having such a messy bedroom.
   A meddles
   B halts
   C chides
   D deflates

I.B Use context clues to determine word meaning

Practice 9: Context Clues

Directions: Read the following sentences. Then choose the best word to fit in the blank. On your answer sheet, darken the circle for the correct answer.

1. Mario poured the precious oil into a _____ and placed it on the shelf.
   A lair
   B vial
   C crag
   D token

2. The voters lost faith in their mayor after the political _____.
   A scandal
   B security
   C minority
   D exposure

3. You can save time if you do your chores in the most _____ way.
   A admirable
   B ignorant
   C exquisite
   D efficient

4. Gretchen enjoys being around people, but her brother is more of a(n) _____ .
   A suspicion
   B occupant
   C introvert
   D identity

5. Students who exhibit _____ behavior may be suspended from school.
   A defiant
   B evident
   C ignorant
   D maximum

6. The message on the answering machine sounded _____ , so it was difficult to understand.
   A annoying
   B crucial
   C forceful
   D garbled

7. The judge was pleased with the jury's _____ decision.
   A faulty
   B favorable
   C gross
   D sparse

8. Since the directions were unclear, there was a great deal of _____ about what to do next.
   A interruption
   B overrule
   C uncertainty
   D confidence

I.B Use context clues to determine word meaning

Practice 10: Multiple-Meaning Words

Directions: Read each numbered sentence. Then choose the correct meaning for the bolded word as it is used in the sentence. On your answer sheet, darken the circle for the correct word.

1. For some people, it is very difficult to **embrace** new ideas.

   A clasp

   B hug

   C accept

   D include

2. The writer's **dispatch** arrived too late to be included in the first edition.

   A haste

   B movement

   C send off

   D report

3. A **mantle** of secrecy surrounded the spy's mission.

   A cloud

   B zone

   C layer

   D shelf

4. The child's **forward** behavior and bad manners surprised the teacher.

   A bold

   B close

   C usual

   D eager

5. I usually save money by purchasing clothes that are on **clearance**.

   A removal

   B space

   C sale

   D permission

6. Young children are **apt** to say the most surprising things at the wrong time.

   A suitable

   B likely

   C intelligent

   D appropriate

7. Mr. Perez gave his wife many small gifts as **tokens** of his affection.

   A indications

   B authorities

   C features

   D currencies

8. His **remote** behavior makes it difficult to converse with him.

   A hidden

   B slight

   C secluded

   D unfriendly

I.C Recognize correct meaning of words with multiple meanings

Practice 11: Multiple-Meaning Words

Directions: Read each numbered sentence. Then choose the correct meaning for the bolded word as it is used in the sentence. On your answer sheet, darken the circle for the correct word.

1. Before signing the contract, the business owner wanted to know the **terms** of the agreement.
   A lengths
   B deadlines
   C conditions
   D equations

2. The watch fit too tightly and left its **impression** on my wrist.
   A imitation
   B imprint
   C publication
   D notion

3. Five days after surgery, the patient was **discharged** from the hospital.
   A relieved
   B acquitted
   C unloaded
   D released

4. As we boarded the roller coaster, my niece **clasped** my hand in fear.
   A hugged
   B fastened
   C gripped
   D hooked

5. Overcoming so many obstacles to the plan truly tested the President's **resolve** to settle the dispute.
   A determination
   B statement
   C separation
   D reduction

6. Joshua has always been honest with me, so I am **inclined** to believe his version of the story.
   A lowered
   B sloped
   C preferred
   D influenced

7. The **passage** from childhood to adulthood presents many challenges and problems.
   A channel
   B transition
   C process
   D permission

8. The community leaders accused the store owner of running a **racket** rather than offering a real service to the people.
   A sports paddle
   B loud distressing noise
   C illegal business
   D livelihood

I.C Recognize correct meaning of words with multiple meanings

Practice 12: Multiple-Meaning Words

Directions: Read each numbered sentence. Then choose the correct meaning for the bolded word as it is used in the sentence. On your answer sheet, darken the circle for the correct word.

1. Ms. Nguyen is our favorite teacher because she is **sensitive** to our needs and problems.

   A   irritative

   B   offensive

   C   registered

   D   responsive

2. On **impulse**, Heather bought five new pairs of shoes and matching purses.

   A   an electrical surge

   B   a motivation

   C   a sudden urge

   D   a strong force

3. The chemistry teacher warned us that there was little **margin** for error if we wanted our experiment to work.

   A   border

   B   blank space

   C   difference

   D   allowance

4. Even though I was not angry, I did need to **vent** my frustrations.

   A   discharge

   B   express

   C   escape

   D   release

5. After investigating the crime scene, the detective offered a detailed **profile** of the criminal.

   A   side view

   B   summary

   C   description

   D   outline

6. The graduates were not interested in the speaker's long, boring **address**.

   A   physical location

   B   formal speech

   C   polite attention

   D   directions

7. In recent years, there have been great **advances** in finding cures for many diseases.

   A   improvements

   B   payments

   C   price increases

   D   promotions

8. People who have many responsibilities must learn how to **delegate** authority to others.

   A   appoint

   B   confer

   C   represent

   D   entrust

I.C   Recognize correct meaning of words with multiple meanings

Practice 13: Synonyms and Antonyms

Directions: For numbers 1–5, find the word that has the same or about the same meaning as the bolded word. On your answer sheet, darken the circle for the correct word.

Directions: For numbers 6–10, find the word that has the opposite meaning of the bolded word. On your answer sheet, darken the circle for the correct word.

1. ideas that **boggle** the mind
   - A frighten
   - B destroy
   - C astonish
   - D refresh

2. many **bothersome** details
   - A hidden
   - B excellent
   - C desirable
   - D annoying

3. **envious** of others' good fortune
   - A contented
   - B jealous
   - C startled
   - D aware

4. living a **solitary** life
   - A social
   - B sensitive
   - C separate
   - D significant

5. an unfortunate **oversight**
   - A belief
   - B vision
   - C mistake
   - D attention

6. **sparse** food supplies
   - A plentiful
   - B scarce
   - C regular
   - D tasty

7. **bewildered** expression
   - A confused
   - B favorable
   - C insensitive
   - D informed

8. **ignorant** of the law
   - A doubtless
   - B mindless
   - C aware
   - D passage

9. **distribute** the materials
   - A issue
   - B collect
   - C share
   - D recycle

10. a **spacious** apartment
   - A redecorated
   - B quiet
   - C cramped
   - D generous

I.D Demonstrate knowledge of synonyms, antonyms, and homophones

Practice 14: Synonyms and Antonyms

Directions: For numbers 1–5, find the word that has the same or about the same meaning as the bolded word. On your answer sheet, darken the circle for the correct word.

1. **elapsed** subscription
   A renewed
   B written
   C planned
   D expired

2. **faulty** electric wires
   A flawed
   B sound
   C installed
   D replaced

3. personal **hygiene**
   A behavior
   B problem
   C cleanliness
   D responsibility

4. an honest **endeavor**
   A mistake
   B occupation
   C attempt
   D opinion

5. **embedded** in your memory
   A released
   B retired
   C exceeded
   D placed

Directions: For numbers 6–10, find the word that has the opposite meaning of the bolded word. On your answer sheet, darken the circle for the correct word.

6. **crucial** information
   A necessary
   B unimportant
   C shared
   D factual

7. **impaired** performance
   A damaged
   B repeated
   C unusual
   D strengthened

8. a **minority** opinion
   A changeable
   B limited
   C majority
   D common

9. **ornamental** decorations
   A elaborate
   B attractive
   C colorful
   D plain

10. **shortage** of volunteers
    A group
    B segment
    C lack
    D surplus

I.D Demonstrate knowledge of synonyms, antonyms, and homophones

Practice 15: Synonyms and Antonyms

Directions: For numbers 1–5, find the word that has the same or about the same meaning as the bolded word. On your answer sheet, darken the circle for the correct word.

Directions: For numbers 6–10, find the word that has the opposite meaning of the bolded word. On your answer sheet, darken the circle for the correct word.

1. a sly **smirk**
   A grin
   B action
   C plan
   D remark

2. **probable** outcome
   A unlikely
   B desired
   C expected
   D final

3. **shriveled** leaves
   A swollen
   B growing
   C withered
   D arranged

4. a troubling **paradox**
   A process
   B puzzle
   C model
   D comment

5. **lofty** mountains
   A distant
   B changing
   C breathtaking
   D towering

6. temporarily **detained**
   A upset
   B accepted
   C released
   D displeased

7. **stationary** bicycle
   A discarded
   B defective
   C convenient
   D mobile

8. **privileged** child
   A resistant
   B unpredictable
   C rowdy
   D disadvantaged

9. constant **discord**
   A disrespect
   B harmony
   C esteem
   D bickering

10. a true **extrovert**
    A companion
    B worrier
    C loner
    D occupant

I.D Demonstrate knowledge of synonyms, antonyms, and homophones

Practice 16: Synonyms and Antonyms

Directions: For numbers 1–5, find the word that has the same or about the same meaning as the bolded word. On your answer sheet, darken the circle for the correct word.

1. **confidential** information
   A available
   B current
   C public
   D restricted

2. **random** events
   A significant
   B designed
   C unplanned
   D formal

3. **surplus** supplies
   A inadequate
   B recycled
   C unnecessary
   D excess

4. **inefficient** service
   A convenient
   B practical
   C disorganized
   D impressive

5. **shimmering** lights
   A glistening
   B dull
   C colorful
   D shattered

Directions: For numbers 6–10, find the word that has the opposite meaning of the bolded word. On your answer sheet, darken the circle for the correct word.

6. **menacing** person
   A dependable
   B generous
   C reassuring
   D incapable

7. **decline** an invitation
   A prevent
   B extend
   C resist
   D accept

8. **ignite** the logs
   A inflame
   B rearrange
   C extinguish
   D agitate

9. **aggressive** behavior
   A remarkable
   B passive
   C offensive
   D respectable

10. **uninhibited** performance
    A symbolic
    B outstanding
    C relaxed
    D reserved

I.D Demonstrate knowledge of synonyms, antonyms, and homophones

Practice 17: Analogies

Directions: Read each analogy. Find the word that correctly completes each analogy. On your answer sheet, darken the circle for the correct word.

1. **Today** is to **tomorrow** as **current** is to _____ .
   A predictable
   B memorable
   C futuristic
   D consequence

2. **Painter** is to **artistic** as **writer** is to _____ .
   A productive
   B literary
   C journal
   D essay

3. **Clock** is to **time** as **map** is to _____ .
   A stationary
   B procession
   C nationality
   D locale

4. **Hospital** is to **medical** as **bank** is to _____ .
   A evident
   B convenient
   C currency
   D financial

5. **Running** is to **hurdle** as **driving** is to _____ .
   A requirement
   B barricade
   C violation
   D overpass

6. **Notes** are to **words** as **melodies** are to _____ .
   A harmony
   B composer
   C lyrics
   D tunes

7. **Courtesy** is to **attention** as **rudeness** is to _____ .
   A interruption
   B suggestion
   C advertisement
   D product

8. **Teacher** is to **educate** as **hostess** is to _____ .
   A decorate
   B impress
   C compromise
   D socialize

I.E   *Choose the correct word to complete an analogy*

Practice 18: Analogies

Directions: Read each analogy. Find the word that correctly completes each analogy. On your answer sheet, darken the circle for the correct word.

1. **Result** is to **causes** as **rating** is to _____ .
   A examinations
   B criteria
   C questions
   D competitions

2. **Opinion** is to **uncertain** as **fact** is to _____ .
   A standard
   B probable
   C unclear
   D doubtless

3. **Celebration** is to **parade** as **emergency** is to _____ .
   A congregate
   B proceed
   C evacuation
   D constrain

4. **Wilting** is to **growing** as **frail** is to _____ .
   A withered
   B harsh
   C hardy
   D confident

5. **Agreement** is to **harmony** as **conflict** is to _____ .
   A suspicion
   B invasion
   C emotion
   D friction

6. **Knife** is to **slice** as **nail** is to _____ .
   A hammer
   B puncture
   C strike
   D drive

7. **Walk** is to **stumble** as **speak** is to _____ .
   A mumble
   B translate
   C stammer
   D repeat

8. **Enemy** is to **attack** as **virus** is to _____ .
   A transmit
   B lessen
   C reform
   D infect

I.E   Choose the correct word to complete an analogy

Practice 19: Analogies

Directions: Read each analogy. Find the word that correctly completes each analogy. On your answer sheet, darken the circle for the correct word.

1. **Doctor** is to **generality** as **surgeon** to _____ .
   A medicine
   B specialty
   C surgery
   D practicality

2. **Disagree** is to **conflict** as **agree** is to _____ .
   A defy
   B endure
   C provoke
   D compromise

3. **Mechanic** is to **tools** as **chef** is to _____ .
   A ingredients
   B preparations
   C kitchens
   D gadgets

4. **Endanger** is to **evil** as **protect** is to _____ .
   A support
   B wisdom
   C welfare
   D relapse

5. **Night** is to **calm** as **morning** is to _____ .
   A listen
   B separate
   C rouse
   D rile

6. **Closed** is to **emptiness** as **open** is to _____ .
   A occupancy
   B vacancy
   C security
   D enclosure

7. **Problem** is to **emergency** as **difficult** is to _____ .
   A dire
   B civil
   C forceful
   D endless

8. **Rude** is to **disrespect** as **polite** is to _____ .
   A elegance
   B emotion
   C equality
   D etiquette

I.E   Choose the correct word to complete an analogy

30

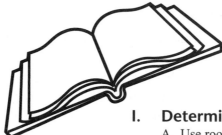

Comprehension

I. Determine the meaning of words in written texts
   A. Use root words and other structural cues to recognize new words
   B. Use context clues to determine word meaning
   C. Recognize correct meaning of words with multiple meanings
   D. Demonstrate knowledge of synonyms and antonyms

II. Identify supporting ideas
   A. Identify relevant facts and details
   B. Use text structure to locate relevant facts and details
   C. Sequence events in chronological order
   D. Follow written directions

III. Summarize a variety of written texts
   A. Determine the main idea or essential message of a text
   B. Paraphrase or summarize the major ideas, themes, or procedures in a text

IV. Perceive relationships and recognize outcomes
   A. Identify cause and effect relationships in a text
   B. Make and verify predictions with information from a text
   C. Connect, compare, and contrast ideas, themes, and issues across texts
   D. Respond to texts by making observations/connections, speculating, questioning, etc.

V. Analyze information in order to make inferences and generalizations
   A. Make and explain inferences
   B. Support interpretations/conclusions with information from a text
   C. Make generalizations based on information from a text

VI. Recognize points of view, propaganda, and statements of fact and opinion
   A. Distinguish fact from opinion in a text
   B. Identify the author's purpose
   C. Recognize logical, ethical, and emotional appeals
   D. Analyze positions, arguments, and evidence presented by an author
   E. Identify bias and propaganda

VII. Read, analyze, and interpret literature
   A. Identify genres of fiction, nonfiction, and poetry
   B. Identify characteristics representative of a given genre
   C. Identify important literary elements
   D. Recognize/interpret figurative language
   E. Recognize use of sound devices

31

1: Do you know how to make recycled paper?

With the right materials and equipment, it really isn't very difficult. You probably won't use the paper for your school assignments. Its **texture** is usually rough, which makes it difficult to fold or use for writing. Nevertheless, making paper can be an enjoyable activity. It is also a good way to learn about making new paper from paper that has already been used in some way. Using recycled paper is an excellent way to save trees.

Materials and Equipment

You will need a stack of old newspapers or other scrap paper. Almost any kind of paper can be used. You can even mix the types of paper you use.

To make a mold, you will need staples or tacks, a wooden frame, and a piece of screening. You can make a wooden frame, but an old picture frame works well. Most hardware stores sell screening, or you can cut a section from a **discarded** screen door or window.

Finally, you need a wash basin, or tub, and an ordinary household blender. Once you have gathered and organized your materials and equipment, you are ready to begin.

Making a Mold

Use the wooden frame, screening, and staples to make the mold. Cut a section of screening that will fit over the wood frame. Staple the screening to the wooden frame. Trim any screening that **extends** from the frame so that you don't cut your fingers during the papermaking process. Your finished mold should look like a small screen window. Set the mold aside until you are ready to use it.

Making Pulp

Take a sheet of newspaper or other scrap paper and tear it into small pieces. The pieces should be about two to three inches long. Fill the blender half full with water, and then put some pieces of paper into the blender. Make sure the paper and water do not fill more than three-fourths of the blender.

Place the lid **securely** on the blender. Blend the paper and water at high speed for several minutes. Blend until the paper and water mix together thoroughly to form a pulp—the thin, moist liquid you will use to make paper.

Making Paper

Place a layer of newspapers on a table or on the floor. The newspapers will catch any drips or spills you make. Set the basin on top of the newspapers.

Take the mold and hold it over the basin. Pour some of the pulp onto the mold. Tilt the mold from side to side so that the pulp can cover the screen. Drain any **excess** water into the basin.

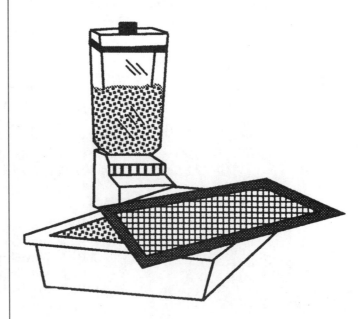

After draining the water, place the mold on a layer of dry newspaper. Place another piece of dry newspaper over the pulp in the mold. Press on the top paper to squeeze out more water. Press out as much water as you can. Then turn the mold over and tap it gently. The molded pulp should drop from the screen onto the newspaper. Let the pulp dry for 24 to 48 hours, until the recycled paper is completely dry. Once it is dry, peel it from the newspaper. Your recycled paper is ready to use.

Using the Paper

Recycled paper will not be as **refined** as the paper you might buy in a store. However, even though your paper is not soft and smooth, you can still use it. Write a letter about the importance of saving the earth's trees. Make a shopping list.

Making Unusual Paper

If you want to make some unusual paper, try using colored paper instead of newspaper. Or add some food coloring to the pulp before pouring it into the mold. Press leaves or flowers into the pulp before it dries. You might even try to "recycle" your recycled paper. Be as creative as you want to be.

Synonyms/Antonyms (I.D)

1. Which word is a SYNONYM for **texture**?

   A Fabric

   B Position

   C Feel

   D Section

Multiple-Meaning Words (I.C)

2. In this passage, the word **discarded** means—

   A shed

   B scratched

   C dismissed

   D thrown out

Structural Cues (I.A)

3. The word **extends** probably comes from the Latin word—

   A *extendere*, meaning "to stretch"

   B *expellere*, meaning "to expel"

   C *exponere*, meaning "to place"

   D *extquirere*, meaning "to search out"

Context Clues (I.B)

4. In this passage, the word **securely** means—

   A loosely

   B freely

   C thoroughly

   D firmly

Synonyms/Antonyms (I.D)

5. Which word is a SYNONYM for **excess**?

   A Shortage

   B Draining

   C Surplus

   D Moist

Multiple-Meaning Words (I.C)

6. In this passage, the word **refined** means—

   A ladylike

   B cleaned

   C smooth

   D polished

Facts/Details (II.A)

7. According to this passage, which of the following is NOT necessary for making recycled paper?

A A household blender

B Leaves and flowers

C Old newspaper

D A wooden frame

Facts/Details (I.A)

8. The thin, moist liquid used to make paper is called—

A mold

B pulp

C texture

D drainage

Text Structure (II.B)

9. To read about the actual steps in making recycled paper, you would read the section titled—

A Materials and Equipment

B Making a Mold

C Making Paper

D Using the Paper

Sequential Order (II.C)

10. Right after stapling the screening to the wooden frame, you should—

A spread newspapers on a table or floor

B trim any screening that extends from the frame

C gather all the materials you will need

D drain the excess water into the basin

Follow Directions (II.D)

11. You prepare the paper for the blender by—

A mixing it with water

B stapling it to the wooden frame

C tearing it into small pieces

D pressing it into the mold

Main Idea (III.A)

12. This passage is mostly about—

A why people should use recycled paper

B why recycled paper feels bumpy and rough

C how to make a wooden frame

D how to make recycled paper

Cause/Effect (IV.A)

13. You should place a layer of newspaper under the basin to—

A protect the furniture or floor from drips and spills

B make the recycled paper stronger

C soften the newspaper and make it easier to tear

D easily tilt the mold above the basin

Inferences (V.A)

14. The author gives enough evidence for you to believe that recycled paper—

A costs less than regular paper

B usually has more imperfections than regular paper

C could be used for school work

D is more beautiful than regular paper

Interpretations/Conclusions (V.B)

15. Tearing the newspaper into small pieces is important because—

A the paper must absorb water

B larger pieces of paper do not fit into the mold

C small pieces of paper fit into the blender better than large pieces of paper

D small pieces of paper create prettier recycled paper

Fact/Opinion (VI.A)

16. Which of the following is a FACT expressed in this passage?

A Using recycled paper is an excellent way to save trees.

B Making paper is an enjoyable activity.

C Making paper is a good way to learn about the process of making new paper from used paper.

D Recycled paper can be used after it has dried completely.

Author's Purpose (VI.B)

17. The author probably wrote this passage to—

A explain why recycled paper should replace regular paper

B show a simple method for making recycled paper

C prove that too many trees are destroyed to make paper

D show that making recycled paper is a difficult process

Author's Positions/Arguments (VI.D)

18. The author of this passage would most likely agree that—

A students should make the paper they use in school

B making paper can be an interesting and enjoyable experience

C few people have the skill to make paper

D recycled paper has few pratical uses

35

19. Write a composition explaining why you would or would not enjoy making paper. Use information from the passage in your composition.

2: It's a Noisy World Out There!

Why are cicadas so noisy?

Cicadas are often mistaken for locusts which are really grasshoppers. But cicadas aren't even closely related to grasshoppers; cicadas are actually relatives of aphids, leafhoppers, and other bugs. And—if you listen closely—you can hear that cicadas make sounds like no other insect around.

Most insects chirp by rubbing their wings together or against another part of their body, such as a leg. But a cicada's sound comes from inside its body. In the lower part of the cicada's thorax (the section where the wings and legs attach) two hollow **cavities** are covered with **membranes,** which act like a drum. Attached to the membranes are muscles that the cicada contracts and releases to beat out its special sound.

But one little cicada can't **orchestrate** the nighttime symphony you typically hear. That sound comes from a group of cicadas.

Here's what happens: Nymphs (immature, wingless cicadas) spend the winter under the ground near the tree roots. When they are mature, they will tunnel up to the surface and latch onto a tree trunk. Then, a mature, winged cicada emerges from the crusty exoskeleton of the nymph. Immediately the males begin to make their distinct sounds to attract females, so they can start the cycle all over again. One type of cicada comes out in such large numbers that people can sometimes hear their **racket** from a mile away!

Why are frogs so noisy?

During spring breeding season, male frogs and toads serenade female frogs with a musical symphony of croaks, squeaks, and buzzes.

There are nearly 3,500 different kinds of frogs in the world, and each species makes its own special sound. Female frogs follow the sounds to where the males are waiting. There could be a lot of different kinds of frogs and toads at a pond or stream during the breeding season. The unique songs help the female find a male frog from her own species.

There are a handful of frogs, though, that don't have eardrums. That's the part of the ear that frogs—and you—need to hear clearly. One species, called Golden Frogs, live near noisy, fast-flowing streams in the forests of Panama.

They make up for their lack of hearing in a couple of ways. The two-inch long Golden Frogs use a kind of sign language to attract mates and protect their territory. For example, they will rotate their front legs in a slow, circular motion at the sight or sound of another Golden Frog.

That's right—although these frogs don't have eardrums, they do recognize sounds. Zoologists think the frogs' lungs, which are located very close to the skin, vibrate the sounds through the frogs' bodies.

If you don't think that's possible, put your hand on a stereo speaker when you are wearing earplugs. You feel the vibrations of the music, even though you can't hear the words—just like the Golden Frogs "hear" sounds around them.

Why do roosters crow in the morning?

Roosters don't crow at dawn to be noisy or annoying. They're protecting their turf!

Before chickens were domesticated, a rooster (the male chicken) traveled with a group of female chickens (hens). The group

37

claimed a particular area as theirs; they raised their families and hunted for food in this territory. The rooster took it upon himself to crow out to any passing birds that this is their spot.

Songbirds do the same thing. It's still pretty dim and cold at dawn, even though the sun is rising. Dim light means birds can't find food very well. On top of that, insects—the preferred food of many birds—don't come out in cold temperatures. Birds don't have much to do until the insects come out, so birds that wander use the time to find a spot for the day.

That's where the singing comes in. Birds that already have a territory—including chickens—sing to send a message to both neighboring birds and passers-by that this is their territory.

So, the next time you hear a rooster crow or a song bird happily chirping in the early morning, you'll know what they are really saying: Keep out!

Why do coyotes and wolves howl?

Coyotes don't intentionally howl at a full moon to scare you. They're just talking to each other. Those mournful **bays** and barks are coyotes' ways of communicating. If you know what to listen for, you can tell apart the cries of coyotes, gray wolves, and red wolves.

Coyotes bark a short, high-pitched howl; red wolves carry **inflection** and melody; and gray wolves mourn a howl that slides down through an octave or more. They can also change the sound, depending on the situation. Different sounds tell all sorts of messages— like they are protecting their turf, sounding to a stray animal, or **rallying** others for a hunt. When wolves are defending their territory,

for example, they are more likely to have a low-pitched, aggressive bark.

If you have dogs at home, this shouldn't surprise you. Dogs are distant cousins of wolves, so they communicate in similar ways. Just like their cousins, dogs can have playful barks or very **aggressive**, protective barks.

Dogs, wolves, and coyotes are social, too. If you need proof, listen closely the next time you hear dogs barking. When one or two dogs start barking in your neighborhood, the rest of the neighborhood dogs usually join the conversation.

Wolves and dogs will also howl along with emergency vehicle sirens. To them, those sirens sound similar to howls. In fact, wildlife biologists often use sirens to locate wild wolf packs.

These passages reprinted with the permission of The Ohio State University's College of Food, Agricultural, and Environmental Studies.

Context Clues (I.B)
1. The word **cavities** means—

   A ears

   B drums

   C holes

   D sections

Structural Cues (I.A)
2. The word **membranes** probably comes from the Latin word—

   A *branca*, meaning "paw"

   B *memor*, meaning "mindful"

   C *membrana*, meaning "skin"

   D *radere*, meaning "to scrape"

Synonyms/Antonyms (I.D)

3. Which word is a SYNONYM for **orchestrate** as it is used in this passage?

   A Arrange

   B Predict

   C Repeat

   D Release

Multiple-Meaning Words (I.C)

4. In this passage, the word **racket** refers to—

   A tennis equipment

   B criminal activity

   C a business

   D noise

Context Clues (I.B)

5. The word **bays** means—

   A territories

   B coyotes

   C fears

   D howls

Context Clues (I.B)

6. The word **inflection** refers to a musical—

   A performance

   B tone

   C protection

   D bark

Synonyms/Antonyms (I.D)

7. Which word is an ANTONYM for **aggressive**?

   A Dangerous

   B Tame

   C Wild

   D Frightening

Synonyms/Antonyms (I.D)

8. Which word is a SYNONYM for **rallying**?

   A Preventing

   B Challenging

   C Gathering

   D Defending

Facts/Details (II.A)

9. An immature cicada is called a—

   A leafhopper

   B aphid

   C thorax

   D nymph

Main Idea (III.A)

10. This passage is mostly about—

    A how different types of creatures communicate with noises

    B how cicadas make noise with their wings and legs

    C why the world is so noisy

    D why some animals communicate better than others

Cause/Effect (IV.A)

11. By making different kinds of sounds, gray wolves—

    A become more protective of their territory

    B communicate with frogs and insects

    C sound more like coyotes and red wolves

    D send different messages to other gray wolves

Connect/Compare/Contrast (IV.C)

12. According to the passage, both cicadas and frogs make sounds to—

A hunt for food

B hide from their enemies

C attract mates

D protect their territory

Connect/Compare/Contrast (IV.C)

13. According to the passage, which group of animals can use sounds to communicate many different kinds of messages?

A Cicadas

B Frogs

C Roosters

D Coyotes and wolves

Interpretations/Conclusions (V.B)

14. Based on information in this passage, which of the following is a reasonable conclusion?

A All insects communicate in the same way.

B Human beings can never understand how animals use sound to communicate.

C Many animals use sound as a way to communicate.

D Scientists have spent little time and effort on understanding the sounds made by animals.

Generalizations (V.C)

15. Which word best describes the sounds made by the creatures discussed in the passage?

A Purposeful

B Creative

C Annoying

D Random

Author's Positions/Arguments (VI.D)

16. Based on information included in the passage, which of the following statements is most reasonable?

A The author believes that scientists waste time by studying the sounds made by animals.

B The author believes that people should learn to communicate with other animals.

C The author believes that studying the communication methods of animals is interesting and worthwhile.

D The author believes that coyotes and wolves have the most developed communication system.

Figurative Language (VII.D)

17. The author says that the rooster "took it upon himself" to crow at passing birds. This means that the rooster—

A carried the other birds from place to place

B hunted for food only in his own territory

C traveled with a group of female chickens

D took responsibility for protecting his territory

Paraphrase/Summarize (III.B)

18. Imagine that a friend asks you what "It's a Noisy World Out There!" is about. What would you tell your friend? Summarize the passage in one paragraph.

Response to Text (IV.D)

19. The author presents information about the sounds made by different creatures. Write a composition that explains how the author's information supports or contradicts what you know about animals and the noises they make. Use specific examples from the text and your own experiences in your answer.

_____

_____

_____

_____

_____

_____

_____

_____

_____

_____

_____

_____

_____

_____

_____

_____

3: Two Poems

Be Like the Bird
by Victor Hugo

Be like the bird, who
Halting in his flight
On limb too **slight**
Feels it give way beneath him,
Yet sings
Knowing he has wings.

The Eagle
by Alfred Lord Tennyson

He **clasps** the crag with crooked hands;
Close to the sea in lonely lands,
Ringed with the azure* world, he stands.

The wrinkled sea beneath him crawls;
He watches from his mountain walls,
And like a thunderbolt he falls.

sky blue

Context Clues (I.B)

1. In "Be Like the Bird," the word **halting**
   means—

   A hiding

   B stopping

   C circling

   D singing

Multiple-Meaning Words (I.C)

2. In "Be Like the Bird," the word **slight**
   means—

   A ignore

   B high

   C weak

   D heavy

Synonyms/Antonyms (I.D)

3. Which word is a SYNONYM for **clasps**
   as it is used in "The Eagle"?

   A Soars

   B Connects

   C Scrapes

   D Grips

Connect/Compare/Contrast (IV.C)

4. Which word best describes both the bird
   in "Be Like the Bird" and the eagle in
   "The Eagle"?

   A Cowardly

   B Gentle

   C Confident

   D Frightening

Interpretations/Conclusions (V.B)

5. Even though the limb gives way beneath him, the bird sings because he knows—

   A the eagle will save him

   B he can fly to safety

   C there are other limbs nearby

   D the limb is not heavy

Figurative Language (VII.D)

6. In "Be Like the Bird," the bird feels the limb "give way beneath him." This means—

   A the bird flies away from the limb

   B the limb bends under the bird's weight

   C the bird stops to rest on the limb

   D the limb weighs too much

Figurative Language (VII.D)

7. The eagle falls "like a thunderbolt." *Like a thunderbolt* is an example of—

   A personification

   B an allusion

   C an idiom

   D a simile

Figurative Language (VII.D)

8. In "The Eagle," the poet states that "the wrinkled sea" crawls beneath the eagle. *The wrinkled sea* is an example of—

   A hyperbole

   B alliteration

   C a metaphor

   D rhyme

Sound Devices (VII.E)

9. Which of the following lines from "The Eagle" contains alliteration?

   A … And like a thunderbolt he falls

   B He watches from his mountain walls …

   C Ringed with the azure world, he stands …

   D He clasps the crag with crooked hands …

Connect/Compare/Contrast (IV.C)

10. Which one of the following words would you use to describe both the bird in Hugo's poem and the eagle in Tennyson's poem?

cowardly   gentle   confident   frightening

Write a paragraph that explains why you would use this word to describe both the bird and the eagle.

_____

_____

_____

_____

_____

_____

_____

_____

_____

_____

_____

_____

_____

Genre Characterisitcs (VII.B); Figurative Language (VII.D)

11. Both "Be Like the Bird" and "The Eagle" are poems. List and explain at least three poetic devices found in either one or both of the poems.

4: Athena and Arachne

The following passage retells the Greek myth about Athena and Arachne.

Athena, Greek goddess of wisdom, spun fine, silken threads and used them to weave splendid cloth with **intricate** designs and brilliant colors. Every day the goddesses from the woods and streams, the nymphs, gathered around Athena to admire her skill and work. They believed she was the finest weaver in all the world. And though she tried to remain humble, Athena herself believed that the work of her hands surpassed all others in beauty.

One day as Athena sat and wove, she heard the nymphs whispering behind her.

"Athena's cloth clearly is the most beautiful." All the nymphs smiled and nodded in agreement. Unaware that Athena could hear them, the nymphs continued their gossip.

"Can you imagine that Arachne would be so bold! Could she truly believe that her cloth is more beautiful than Athena's work?"

When Athena heard what the nymphs said, she flew into a rage.

"How dare Arachne say her cloth is more beautiful than mine!" Athena grabbed her shawl and wrapped it over her head and across her face. She grabbed a cane and bent herself over like an old woman. In this disguise, she planned to visit Arachne and settle the matter at once.

When Athena found her, Arachne was busily engaged in her weaving. Her hands moved swiftly, skillfully as she toiled over a multi-colored fabric of **exquisite** beauty. So **preoccupied** was Arachne with her work, that she did not see Athena approach her.

"Young woman, you weave a very lovely cloth. You must have learned your art from Athena, the finest weaver of all." Athena stared straight at Arachne as she spoke.

"Athena has nothing to teach me, old woman! She believes she is the finest weaver, but her time has passed. I am the finest weaver in the world. Indeed, Athena could learn from me!" Arachne laughed as she spoke to Athena.

"So, you could teach me about weaving, Arachne?" Athena pulled the shawl from her head and dropped her cane on the floor. When she realized that it was Athena who stood before her, Arachne hung her head in shame.

Still Athena stormed against Arachne. "I challenge you to prove yourself in a weaving contest!"

"Oh, no, Athena. I did not mean what I said. Surely you are still ..."

"It is too late, Arachne. Now you must live up to your boasts and claims."

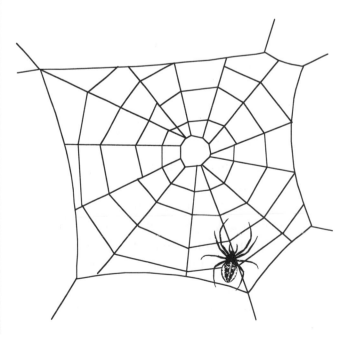

47

So, Athena and Arachne set to work, each determined to outdo the other. Quickly, skillfully, both women created their works of art. Using only the finest threads with the most brilliant colors, Athena wove a cloth **depicting** the twelve greatest gods and goddesses. When finished, she sat back and admired her work. Then Athena held it up so the nymphs, who had followed her and hid just outside the window, could see her handiwork as they peaked inside. The nymphs simply stood in awe, so beautiful was Athena's work.

On the other side of the room, Arachne toiled over her own cloth, using only the most perfect threads of only the purest colors. Like Athena's, Arachne's fabric depicted the twelve greatest gods and goddesses, but her cloth also included scenes of their most magnificent deeds and achievements, revealing even the most **minute** details. Finally, Arachne finished, turned to Athena, and held up her work. The nymphs, still peaking through the window, gasped. Before considering the consequences of her words, one nymph blurted out what everyone was thinking.

"What splendid fabric! How breathtaking! Surely there is no finer..." Catching a glimpse of Athena, the nymph said no more. There was little doubt that Arachne had woven exceptional fabric, superior to any that had ever come from Athena's loom.

Once again, Athena raged. Screaming at Arachne, she slashed her rival's magnificent work into shreds. Fearing that she might be shredded as well, Arachne huddled behind her loom to escape Athena's rage, but Athena saw her. Reaching behind the loom, Athena touched Arachne's forehead with her fingertips.

"You shall never compete with me again, but I can assure you of one thing. You, dear Arachne, will weave until the end of time."

Hearing Athena's words, Arachne felt a searing bolt of heat and pain surge through her body. Her nose and ears shriveled and plopped to the floor, and her hair fell out in clumps. Burning and itching, her fingers grew longer and bent at the joints; her thumbs snapped off and rolled across the floor. In just seconds, Arachne's fingers were **transformed** into eight thin, hairy legs. In horror, the nymphs shielded their eyes and turned away from the window. Arachne, now a helpless spider, crawled up the wall and began spinning her first web.

Synonyms/Antonyms (I.D)
1. Which word is an ANTONYM for **intricate**?
   A Appealing
   B Complex
   C Uninvolved
   D Repeated

Context Clues (I.B)
2. In this passage, the word **exquisite** means—
   A excellent
   B skillful
   C swift
   D woven

Context Clues (I.A)
3. In this passage, the word **preoccupied** means—
   A neglectful
   B disinterested
   C absorbed in thought
   D jealous

Synonyms/Antonyms (I.D)

4. Which word is a SYNONYM for **depicting** as it is used in this passage?

A Weaving

B Following

C Describing

D Showing

Context Clues (I.B)

5. In this passage, the word **minute** means—

A perfect

B magnificent

C tiny

D pure

Structural Cues (I.A)

6. The word **transformed** probably comes from the Latin word—

A *fama*, meaning "fame"

B *faber*, meaning "worker"

C *fortis*, meaning "strong"

D *formare*, meaning "to form or shape"

Facts/Details (II.A)

7. Athena disguises herself as a(n)—

A nymph

B goddess

C old woman

D spider

Sequential Order (II.C)

8. Arachne hides behind her loom—

A as soon as Athena arrives

B right after Athena slashes her work

C right after Athena removes her disguise

D just before she and Athena have their weaving contest

Paraphrase/Summarize (III.B)

9. Which is the best summary of this passage?

A Arachne proves she is a better weaver than Athena.

B Threatened by Arachne's talent, Athena solves the problem.

C Athena teaches the nymphs how to spin and weave.

D The nymphs cause problems between Athena and Arachne.

Cause/Effect (IV.A)

10. Arachne brags to Athena because she—

A doesn't recognize Athena in her disguise

B wants Athena to challenge her to a contest

C knows her bragging will make Athena angry

D wants Athena to admit that Arachne is the better weaver

Interpretations/Conclusions (V.B)

11. Athena probably suggests a weaving contest because she—

A wants to give Arachne a chance to weave the better cloth

B wants the nymphs to see how Arachne weaves

C believes she can weave a finer cloth than Arachne

D wants to change Arachne into a spider

Generalizations (V.C)

12. Both Athena and Arachne could be described as—

   A forgiving

   B ungrateful

   C conceited

   D magnificent

Identify Genre (VII.A)

13. In which section of the library would "Athena and Arachne" most likely be?

   A Reference

   B Literature

   C Arts

   D History

Genre Characteristics (VII.B)

14. Which of the following elements found in "Athena and Arachne" are also elements of mythology?

   A Greek characters

   B Conflict between two characters

   C A character that changes from human to animal form

   D Dialogue among characters

Literary Elements (VII.C)

15. The main conflict in this passage is between—

   A Arachne and the nymphs

   B Athena and the nymphs

   C the gods and goddesses

   D Athena and Arachne

Literary Elements (VII.C)

16. Which word best describes the relationship between the characters Athena and Arachne?

   A Competitive

   B Cooperative

   C Supportive

   D Sensitive

Response to Text (IV.D); Literary Elements (VII.C)

17. Choose three words to describe Athena. Complete the diagram below by writing each word in one of the boxes. Then find specific examples from the story that support each description of Athena.

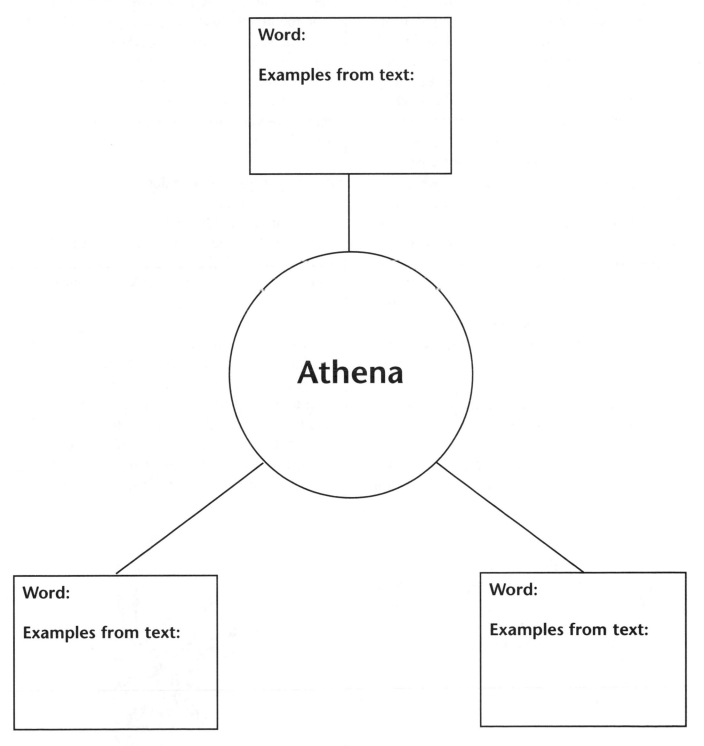

5: Along Came a Spider

How do you react when you see a spider? Some people panic and run away in terror when they see one nearby. This is unfortunate because spiders are actually very interesting creatures. Although some kinds of spiders are poisonous, most spiders rarely **pose** a threat to people. Most importantly, however, spiders provide a valuable service in nature because they eat insects. Without spiders, these other creepy crawlers might overrun us.

Why do spiders frighten so many people? At a close look, spiders do look rather **ferocious**. Many are "furry" like mammals, others have sharp, threatening fangs, and some have dozens of eyes. In addition to their **menacing** appearance, spiders are often the "bad guys" in many children's stories and rhymes. It is also true that a few spiders, like the black widow and brown recluse, are poisonous. However, even these spiders rarely bite people.

For the most part, **ignorance**, or a lack of knowledge, about spiders causes the fear. If people learn more about spiders and their ways of life, they are less likely to fear these little creatures. In fact, spiders are really fascinating. Learning more about them can change a person's whole attitude about these creatures.

There are more than 30,000 kinds of spiders on earth. The first thing to know about spiders is that they are not insects. They belong to a group of animals known as arachnids. Scientists divide spiders into two main groups. Web builders, as their name suggests, are spiders that build webs to catch their food. Wandering spiders hunt for their food on the ground.

A spider's body has two main **segments**: the cephalothorax (the front part) and the abdomen (the rear part). A spider's eyes, mouth, and legs are part of its cephalothorax. The mouth includes two jaws, each with a fang that can secrete poison. Most spiders have eight eyes, but some have fewer (even one!). Spiders have eight legs attached to the cephalothorax, which has a hard covering called the carapace. This covering serves as the spider's skeleton.

A spider's abdomen does not have a covering, so it is softer than the cephalothorax. The abdomen holds several body organs, including the spider's heart and silk glands. A spider makes silk inside its abdomen. At the very back of the spider's body are spinnerets, where the silk exits the body.

Depending on the kind of spider, a mother spider might lay more than 100 eggs. The female spins a silk sac and lays her eggs in it. Some female spiders simply guard the sac from enemies, but others, like wolf spiders, actually carry the sac on their back. Mother wolf spiders also carry the **spiderlings** on their back, but most baby spiders are left on their own.

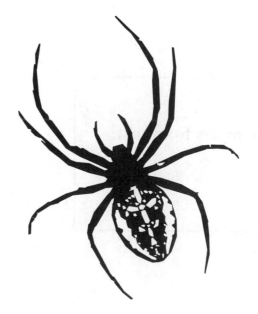

Multiple-Meaning Words (I.C)

1. In this passage, the word **pose** means—

   A sit

   B attitude

   C speak

   D present

Context Clues (I.B)

2. The word **ferocious** means—

   A fierce

   B gentle

   C natural

   D poisonous

Synonyms/Antonyms (I.D)

3. Which word is an ANTONYM for **menacing** as it is used in this passage?

   A Rare

   B Creepy

   C Calming

   D Humorous

Structural Cues (I.A)

4. The word **ignorance** probably comes from the Latin word—

   A *gerere*, meaning "to carry"

   B *ignis*, meaning "fire"

   C *ignorare*, meaning "not to know"

   D *gratis*, meaning "thankful"

Synonyms/Antonyms (I.D)

5. Which word is a SYNONYM for **segment**?

   A Thorax

   B Abdomen

   C Section

   D Skeleton

Context Clues (I.B)

6. The word **spiderlings** refers to—

   A parts of a spider's body

   B spinnerets

   C spider eggs

   D baby spiders

Facts/Details (II.A)

7. The hard covering on the spider's cephalothorax is called the—

   A carapace

   B sac

   C abdomen

   D segment

Facts/Details (II.A)

8. A spider's silk exits its body through the—

   A organ

   B abdomen

   C cephalothorax

   D spinnerets

Main Idea (III.A)

9. The second paragraph is mostly about—

   A people's reasons for fearing spiders

   B why spiders are dangerous

   C which spiders are poisonous to people

   D the appearance of dangerous spiders

Cause/Effect (IV.A)

10. According to the passage, people often fear spiders because they—

    A have been bitten by spiders in the past

    B know most spiders are very dangerous

    C do not have accurate information about spiders

    D know that spiders hunt for their food

Inferences (V.A)

11. Mother wolf spiders protect their young by—

A building webs on the ground

B carrying their egg sacs and spiderlings on their backs

C laying more than 100 eggs

D making silk in their abdomens

Generalizations (V.C)

12. People who know a great deal about spiders probably would describe them as—

A poisonous

B frightening

C overly protective

D generally harmless

Fact/Opinion (VI.A)

13. Which is an OPINION expressed in this passage?

A Spiders are fascinating creatures.

B There are more than 30,000 kinds of spiders on earth.

C A spider produces silk inside its abdomen.

D The carapace serves as the spider's skeleton.

Author's Positions/Arguments (VI.D)

14. The author of this passage seems to believe that spiders are—

A useless to people

B frightening creatures

C poor hunters

D interesting creatures to study

Recognize Author's Appeals (VI.C)

15. The author tries to lessen the reader's fear of spiders by—

A explaining why black widow and brown recluse spiders are dangerous to people

B explaining what would happen if there were no spiders in the world

C providing factual information about spiders' appearance and behavior

D poking fun at people who panic when they see spiders

Bias/Propaganda (VI.E)

16. Which statement uses the propaganda technique called "name calling"?

A Most importantly, however, spiders provide a valuable service in nature because they eat insects.

B Learning more about them can change a person's whole attitude about them.

C Without spiders, these other creepy crawlers might overrun us.

D For the most part, ignorance, or a lack of knowledge, about spiders causes the fear.

Connect/Compare/Contrast (IV.C); Response to Text (IV.D)

17. Think about the story "Athena and Arachne" and the passage "Along Came a Spider." Given what you learned about spiders and how some people fear them, do you think Athena chose an appropriate way to punish Arachne? Write a composition that explains your stand.

6: A Simple Way to Save Lives

Choking is the sixth leading cause of accidental death. It is also an emergency situation that often can be treated without the aid of a medical professional. In a few minutes, almost anyone can learn to perform the Heimlich **maneuver**, a technique that has saved thousands of lives.

The Heimlich maneuver was developed by Dr. Henry Heimlich, after studies showed that even while choking, a person still has a substantial amount of air in the lungs. An upward thrust on the diaphragm compresses the lungs and forces the air out through the esophagus. About one quart of air is **expelled** from the mouth in a quarter of a second. This sharp burst of air literally pops an **obstruction** out of the throat.

The first step in the Heimlich maneuver is recognizing how a choking victim looks and acts. Often, choking victims are mistaken for heart attack victims. Since choking and heart attacks need very different kinds of treatment, it is important to know the following symptoms of choking:

- A choking victim has trouble breathing and cannot speak. Most heart attack victims can both breathe and speak.
- A choking victim turns blue. This is due to a lack of oxygen in the body tissues.
- A choking victim becomes unconscious because there is no oxygen reaching the brain.

Another clue to choking is the setting. About 90% of choking victims are eating when choking occurs. Choking is the cause of 98% of people who become unconscious and die in or near a restaurant.

Today, many people know the universal "choking sign"—the victim grasps the throat with the hand. If a person gives that sign, others should ask, "Are you choking?" Although choking victims are unable to answer, they can probably respond by nodding.

Once choking is recognized as the problem, the Heimlich maneuver should be applied quickly. A choking person has enough oxygen to survive only about four minutes. The maneuver can be used whether the victim is standing, sitting, or lying down. It is also possible to perform the Heimlich maneuver on oneself.

Standing

Stand behind the victim and wrap your arms around the person's waist. Make a fist and place the thumb side against the victim's abdomen. Make sure your fist is slightly above the navel and below the rib cage. Grasp your fist with your other hand and press into the victim's abdomen with a quick, upward thrust. Repeat the procedure several times to **dislodge** the obstruction.

Be careful not to squeeze the chest because that can cause fractured ribs, a crushed chest, or fatal internal injuries. You should apply pressure to the abdomen, not the chest, by bending your arms at the elbow.

Sitting

If a choking victim is sitting, apply the maneuver in exactly the same way as when a victim is standing. Before administering the procedure, stand or kneel by the victim's chair so that your arms fit easily around the victim's waist.

Lying Down

If a choking victim is lying down, do not waste time trying to elevate the fallen victim. You can easily perform the Heimlich maneuver while the victim is **supine**. First, turn the victim on his or her back, face upward. Then face the victim and kneel **astride** the victim's hips. Make sure your hands are above the navel and below the rib cage. Press the victim's abdomen with a quick, upward thrust. Repeat if necessary.

Self-Administration

If you are choking and no one is there to assist you, you can perform the Heimlich maneuver on yourself. Place the thumb side of your fist into the abdomen. Grasp your fist with your other hand. Press your abdomen with a quick, upward thrust, just as you would if you were trying to save someone else. You can also save yourself from choking by leaning into the edge of a chair, sink, table, or other stationary object. Press your abdomen into the object in the same way as you would otherwise place your fist—slightly above the navel and below the rib cage.

Knowing the simple steps in performing the Heimlich maneuver will let you react quickly in an emergency situation. You never know when you might use your **expertise** to save a life.

Important Note: Before administering the Heimlich maneuver, a person should receive proper training from an expert in the procedure. This passage provides only a general description of the life-saving technique.

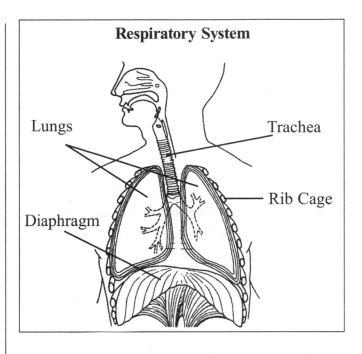

Respiratory System

Lungs — Trachea — Rib Cage — Diaphragm

Context Clues (I.B)

1. In this passage, the word **maneuver** means—

   A removal

   B compression

   C emergency

   D technique

Structural Cues (I.A)

2. The word **expelled** probably comes from the Latin word—

   A *expendere*, meaning "to spend out"

   B *expellere*, meaning "to drive out"

   C *expendere*, meaning "to pay out"

   D *expidere*, meaning "to make ready"

Synonyms/Antonyms (I.D)

3. Which word is a SYNONYM for **obstruction**?

   A Esophagus

   B Burst

   C Blockage

   D Thrust

Context Clues (I.B)

4. In this passage, the word **dislodge** means—

    A dislocate

    B examine

    C remove

    D proceed

Context Clues (I.B)

5. In this passage, the word **supine** means—

    A choking

    B moving backwards

    C standing

    D lying on the back

Structural Cues (I.A)

6. In this passage, the word **astride** means—

    A beside

    B across

    C behind

    D at

Synonyms/Antonyms (I.D)

7. Which word is a SYNONYM for **expertise**?

    A observation

    B reaction

    C skill

    D situation

Facts/Details (II.A)

8. To perform the Heimlich maneuver, you thrust upward on a person's—

    A esophagus

    B lungs

    C diaphragm

    D ribs

Sequential Order (II.C)

9. To help a choking victim who is standing, what should you do right after wrapping your arms around the person's waist?

    A Press the victim's abdomen quickly.

    B Turn the victim so you can see the person's face.

    C Make a fist and place the thumb side against the victim's abdomen.

    D Apply gentle pressure to the victim's abdomen.

Follow Directions (II.D)

10. Which of the following should you NOT do when using the Heimlich maneuver?

    A Squeeze the victim's chest.

    B Repeat the procedure.

    C Use the procedure on yourself.

    D Ask the person if he or she is choking.

Main Idea (III.A)

11. The second paragraph is mostly about—

    A how to recognize a choking victim

    B how the Heimlich maneuver came to be

    C how people breathe and swallow

    D why the Heimlich maneuver can be done quickly

Cause/Effect (IV.A)

12. It is important to recognize the difference between choking victims and heart attack victims because—

A only medical professionals can help choking victims

B some choking victims may be having a heart attack

C a heart attack victim needs a different kind of care than a choking victim

D their symptoms are exactly the same

Interpretations/Conclusions (V.B)

13. According to the diagram, a person's diaphragm is located—

A between the lungs

B on the left side of the body

C beside the trachea

D beneath the lungs

Interpretations/Conclusions (V.B)

14. According to the the diagram, which part of the body is blocked when a person is choking?

A Lungs

B Rib cage

C Trachea

D Diaphragm

Author's Purpose (VI.B)

15. The author of this passage probably wrote it in order to—

A persuade readers to learn more about choking victims

B prove that only medical professionals can help victims in an emergency

C describe one procedure for helping a choking victim

D explain how a person breathes

Fact/Opinion (VI.A)

16. Which is an OPINION expressed in this passage?

A Anyone can learn to perform the Heimlich maneuver.

B The Heimlich maneuver can be used to save choking victims.

C A choking victim has trouble breathing.

D The Heimlich maneuver can be performed on a victim who is sitting.

Bias/Propaganda (VI.E)

17. The author states that "You never know when you might use your expertise to save a life." Which of the following common sayings expresses a similar idea?

A Haste makes waste.

B One good act deserves another.

C A little knowledge is a dangerous thing.

D Be prepared.

18. The author believes readers should learn the Heimlich maneuver. Write a composition that summarizes the evidence offered by the author to support her view.

_____

_____

_____

_____

_____

_____

_____

_____

_____

_____

_____

_____

_____

_____

_____

_____

Response to Text (IV.D)

19. Write a composition that explains why you would or would not be willing to learn the Heimlich maneuver. Use information from the text in your answer.

_____

_____

_____

_____

_____

_____

_____

_____

_____

_____

_____

_____

_____

_____

_____

_____

_____

7: The Wind in a Frolic

The following passage is taken from "The Wind in a Frolic" by William Howitt.

Words you should know—
commotion (disorder; disturbance)
squalls (wind storms)
lustier (stronger)
urchins (youngsters)

1   The wind one morning sprung up from sleep,
2   Saying, "Now for a **frolic**! Now for a leap!
3   Now for a **madcap**, galloping chase!
4   I'll make a commotion in every place!"
5   So it swept with a bustle right up through a great town,
6   Creaking the signs, and scattering down
7   Shutters; and whisking, with merciless squalls,
8   Old women's bonnets and gingerbread stalls.
9   There never was heard a much lustier shout,
10 As the apples and oranges **trundled** about;
11 And the urchins, that stand with their thievish eyes
12 Forever on watch, ran off each with a prize.

13 Then away to the field it went blustering and humming,
14 And the cattle all wondered whatever was coming;
15 It plucked by their tails the grave, matronly cows,
16 And tossed the colts' manes all about their brows,
17 Till, offended at such a familiar salute,
18 They all turned their backs, and stood sullenly mute.
19 So on it went, **capering** and playing its pranks:
20 Whistling with reeds on the broad river's banks;
21 Puffing the birds as they sat on the spray,
22 Or the traveler grave on the king's highway.
23 It was not too nice to hustle the bags
24 Of the beggar, and flutter his dirty rags:
25 'Twas so bold, that it feared not to play its joke
26 With the doctor's wig, or the gentleman's cloak.
27 Through the forest it roared, and cried gaily, "Now,
28 You sturdy old oaks, I'll make you bow!"
29 And it made them bow without much ado,
30 Or it cracked their great branches through and through.

31	Then it rushed like a monster on cottage and farm,
32	Striking their dwellings with sudden alarm;
33	And they ran out like bees in a midsummer swarm.
34	There were dames with their 'kerchiefs tied over their caps,
35	To see if their poultry were free from mishaps;
36	The turkeys they gobbled, the geese screamed aloud,
37	And the hens crept to roost in a terrified crowd;
38	There was rearing of ladders, and logs laying on
39	Where the thatch from the roof threatened soon to be gone.
40	But the wind had passed on, and had met in a lane,
41	With a schoolboy, who panted and struggled in vain;
42	For it tossed him, and twirled him, then passed, and he stood,
43	With his hat in a pool, and his shoe in the mud.

Context Clues (I.B)

1. The word **frolic** refers to a—

A presentation

B storm

C playful activity

D ceremony

Synonyms/Antonyms (I.D)

2. Which word is an ANTONYM for **madcap**?

A Calm

B Faraway

C Different

D Wild

Context Clues (I.B)

3. In this passage, the word **trundled** means—

A rolled

B fell

C grew

D disappeared

Synonyms/Antonyms (I.D)

4. Which word is a SYNONYM for **capering**?

A Resting

B Jumping

C Cringing

D Standing

Sequential Order (II.C)

5. After blowing through the town (lines 5–12), the wind moves on to—

A the king's highway

B the forest

C the river's bank

D the field

Cause/Effect (IV.A)

6. The schoolboy's hat ends up in a pool (line 43) because—

A he tosses it there before running away

B the wind blows it from his head

C the beggar steals it from him

D he wants to hide it from the wind

Inferences (V.A)

7. The colts turn their backs (line 18) because they want to—

    A face away from the wind

    B watch for the wind

    C play with the wind

    D look for the cattle

Generalizations (V.C)

8. Which word best describes the wind's actions in this passage?

    A Calming

    B Productive

    C Delightful

    D Disruptive

Genre Characteristics (VII.B)

9. This passage would most likely appear in—

    A a science text book

    B a literature collection

    C a weather almanac

    D a news magazine

Sound Devices (VII.E)

10. In line 7, the author describes the wind as "whisking." The word *whisking* sounds like a noise made by the wind. This is an example of—

    A personification

    B assonance

    C onomatopoeia

    D hyperbole

Figurative Language (VII.D)

11. Which line from the poem includes a simile?

    A The wind one morning sprung up from sleep…

    B I'll make a commotion in every place!

    C 'Twas so bold, that it feared not to play its joke…

    D Then it rushed like a monster on cottage and farm…

64

Genre Characteristics (VII.B); Figurative Language (VII.D)

12. "The Wind in a Frolic" is a poem. List and explain at least three example of poetic devices found in "The Wind in a Frolic."

_____

_____

_____

_____

_____

_____

_____

_____

_____

_____

_____

_____

_____

_____

_____

_____

_____

Figurative Language (VII.D)

13. How does the poet use personification throughout "The Wind in a Frolic"? In a composition, list and explain at least three examples of personification from the poem.

_____

_____

_____

_____

_____

_____

_____

_____

_____

_____

_____

_____

_____

_____

_____

_____

66

8: A Tree from the Past

Have you ever seen a ginkgo tree? If you have, then you have seen the oldest type of tree known to live on earth. Perhaps as old as 280 million years, the ginkgo stands as a true survivor in the tree world. The ginkgo also has characteristics that make it one of the most fascinating trees in the world.

Characteristics

The ginkgo tree's scientific name is *Ginkgo biloba*. It is classified as a conifer (a tree that makes cones), but it is not like most conifers. Most conifers are evergreen, keeping their green leaves (needles) all year. The ginkgo tree, on the other hand, loses its leaves in the fall. For this reason, it is also a **deciduous** tree. Deciduous trees lose their leaves in the fall of the year.

The average ginkgo tree stands 60 to 80 feet tall, but some can grow as tall as 120 feet. The tree has unique, fan-shaped leaves that are about three inches long and six inches wide. Each leaf has two lobes and parallel veins. The leaves grow on long shoots. The unique appearance of the ginkgo's leaves makes them easy to identify. Because the tree's leaves look like a maidenhair fern, the ginkgo is sometimes called the "maidenhair tree." During the warm months, the leaves have a dark green color, but they turn a bright, **shimmering** yellow in the fall before they drop from the tree.

There are both male and female ginkgo trees, and each type produces a different kind of cone. The male tree has many small cones, while the female has small single cones or small pairs of cones. The female's cones produce a yellowish-orange, plum-shaped fruit which has two layers. The thick, fleshy outer layer surrounds the hard **kernel** on the inside. The kernel is quite tasty if it is roasted, but the fruit's outer layer has a strong, offensive odor.

When female trees drop their fruits in the fall, the smell can be quite disgusting. It is easy to understand why the ginkgo tree has earned the title of "stink bomb tree" in some places—and why male ginkgoes are more popular than female ones.

History of the Ginkgo Tree

Scientists have found fossil remains of the ginkgo tree that **predate** the glaciers. Long before the glaciers moved across the land and chilled the weather, members of the ginkgo family grew throughout the mild climates of both the Northern and Southern Hemispheres. At one time, there were probably 50 different types of ginkgo trees growing in the world. Today only one type of ginkgo tree remains, and it does not grow in the wild. What happened to this family of trees that was once so plentiful and widespread?

At four times during the earth's history, glaciers grew and spread across the land. Some glaciers were a mile thick. Although they moved only inches per day, their size made them very destructive. They destroyed whatever was in their path. The glaciers' growth also brought a severe drop in

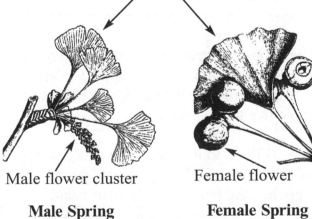

Fan-shaped leaves with 2 lobes

Male flower cluster

Female flower

Male Spring Branchlet

Female Spring Branchlet

temperatures. Only trees that grew in mild climates, still out of the glaciers' reach, survived the force and cold weather. When the glaciers retreated for the last time, the ginkgo tree survived only in southeastern China.

Ginkgo trees might have disappeared completely if the Chinese and Japanese people had not taken an interest in them. The Chinese people admired the trees for their beauty. They also ate the kernels found in the ginkgo's fruit. The Chinese people began to grow ginkgo trees so they could harvest the tasty kernels. They used some substances from the tree in medicines. Eventually the Chinese planted ginkgo trees around their temples and used the fruit in religious ceremonies. In China, ginkgo trees more than 1000 years old still grow in some temple gardens.

Japanese visitors to China admired the ginkgo trees, also. Sometime during the sixth century, Japanese priests took some of the trees from China to Japan. Like the Chinese people, the Japanese people planted the trees around their temples.

The Ginkgo Tree in the Modern World

Ginkgo trees first came to the United States in the late 1700s. They were planted in Philadelphia. Since Americans liked the ginkgoes, they soon appeared in other places in the country. The ginkgo trees continue to be quite popular in many places today. They are used as **ornamental** trees in parks, gardens, and yards across the United States because people like their appearance.

In addition to its beauty, the ginkgo offers other benefits as well. In general, the ginkgo is a very healthy tree, particularly resistant to insects and disease. It can also **tolerate** pollution and drought, which makes it well

suited for today's world. Long ago the Chinese people discovered that the ginkgo tree could be used in medicines. Modern researchers use a substance from the tree to make asthma medicine and continue to investigate its other healing qualities.

Conclusion

The ginkgo tree is certainly one of the most interesting trees in the world. As the last survivor of its family, this ancient tree gives us a glimpse deep into the past. Perhaps Charles Darwin named it correctly when he called it a *living fossil*.

Context Clues (I.B)
1. In this passage, the word **deciduous** refers to trees that—

    A make cones

    B have lived since the time of glaciers

    C lose their leaves in the fall

    D remain green all year

Synonyms/Antonyms (I.D)
2. Which word is a SYNONYM for **shimmering**?

    A Flowing

    B Glowing

    C Colorful

    D Fascinating

Multiple-Meaning Words (I.C)
3. In this passage, the word **kernel** means—

    A central meaning

    B small piece

    C cone

    D seed

Structural Cues (I.A)

4. In this passage, the word **predate** means—

A come before

B survive

C exist in a mild climate

D grow in the wild

Structural Cues (I.A)

5. In this passage, the word **ornamental** means—

A popular

B healthy

C temporary

D decorative

Multiple-Meaning Words (I.C)

6. In this passage, the word **tolerate** means—

A understand

B allow

C withstand

D care

Facts/Details (II.A)

7. The ginkgo tree's kernel grows—

A inside a cone

B in two layers

C inside its fruit

D only on male trees

Text Structure (II.B)

8. In which section of the passage would you look for information on the average size of ginkgo trees?

A Conclusion

B The Ginkgo Tree in the Modern World

C History of the Ginkgo Tree

D Characteristics

Sequential Order (II.C)

9. According to the passage, which of the following happened first?

A Ginkgo trees first came to the United States.

B Many ginkgo trees were destroyed by glaciers.

C The Chinese people planted ginkgo trees around their temples.

D The Japanese priests planted ginkgo trees around their temples.

Main Idea (III.A)

10. The seventh paragraph is mostly about—

A how glaciers destroyed the ginkgo trees

B why the ginkgo tree survived the glaciers

C old ginkgo trees found near Chinese temples

D how the Chinese people have used the ginkgo tree

Cause/Effect (IV.A)

11. According to this passage, male ginkgo trees are more popular than female ginkgo trees because—

  A male ginkgo trees do not produce fruit that smells offensive

  B female ginkgo trees take too long to grow

  C female ginkgo trees do not produce enough cones

  D male ginkgo trees have more attractive leaves

Predictions (IV.B)

12. Based on information in this passage, which of the following is most likely to happen?

  A Ginkgo trees will disappear from the earth within 50 years.

  B Ginkgo trees will continue to be popular for their beauty, resistance to disease, and medical uses.

  C All ginkgo trees will be removed from gardens, parks, and yards in the United States.

  D Scientists will discover another type of ginkgo tree in northern China.

Inferences (V.A)

13. The ginkgo trees in southeastern China survived because—

  A the Chinese people had planted more of them in that area

  B the glaciers did not reach that part of China

  C the strongest ginkgo trees grew in that area

  D the glaciers that reached that area were not as destructive as others

Interpretations/Conclusions (V.B)

14. According to the diagram, which of the following is true?

  A The flowers on male and female ginkgo trees look the same.

  B Flowers are formed on the male ginkgo tree's leaves.

  C The leaves on male and female trees both have two lobes.

  D The male ginkgo tree's flowers have one bud.

Interpretations/Conclusions (V.B)

15. The author of this passage gives enough evidence for you to believe that—

  A only trees in the ginkgo family failed to survive the glaciers

  B many types of plants probably disappeared as a result of the glaciers

  C ginkgo trees will probably lose popularity in the United States

  D ginkgo trees are stronger than any other trees on earth

Author's Purpose (VI.B)

16. The author probably wrote this passage to—

  A encourage people to plant ginkgo trees

  B explain why people do not like female ginkgo trees

  C explain the history and unique characteristics of the ginkgo tree

  D show how glaciers destroyed plants on earth

Recognize Author's Appeals (VI.C)

17. The author states that Charles Darwin probably named the ginkgo tree "correctly when he called it a *living fossil*" in order to—

   A convince the reader that ginkgo trees survived the glaciers

   B show that Charles Darwin knew a great deal about trees

   C show that ginkgo trees have unusual characteristics

   D stress that the ginkgo tree is an ancient tree which has survived until modern times

Bias/Propaganda (VI.E)

18. The author calls the ginkgo tree a "true survivor" to emphasize that the tree—

   A has unusual leaves and cones

   B now grows in several countries

   C grows well in both mild and cold climates

   D is one of the oldest types of tree on earth

Fact/Opinion (VI.A)

19. Which of the following is an OPINION expressed in this passage?

   A The average ginkgo tree stands 60 to 80 feet tall.

   B There are both male and female ginkgo trees.

   C The ginkgo tree is one of the most interesting trees in the world.

   D The Chinese people ate the kernels found in the ginkgo tree's fruit.

Response to Text (IV.D)

20a. Think of another type of tree other than a ginkgo. How is a ginkgo tree similar to this tree? How is a ginkgo tree different from this tree? Record your ideas on the Venn diagram below.

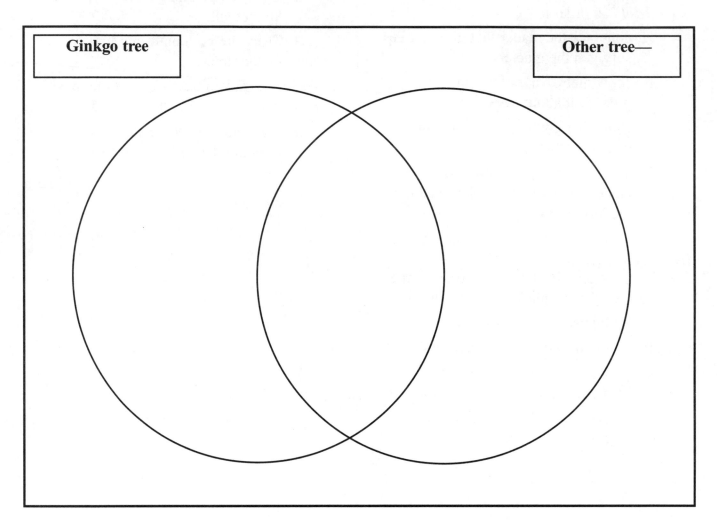

72

Paraphrase/Summarize (III.B)

20b. Using information recorded on the Venn diagram, summarize your ideas about the ginkgo tree and explain how it is **similar** to the other tree you considered.

_____

_____

_____

_____

_____

_____

_____

_____

_____

_____

_____

_____

_____

_____

_____

_____

_____

_____

©ECS Learning Systems, Inc.

9: Follow the Bouncing Ball

Do you know why some balls bounce better than others? For example, a golf ball doesn't bounce as well as the little "super ball" that you can buy in a toy store. Since a golf ball and a "super ball" are both balls, you might expect them to bounce in the same way, but they don't. A ball's bounce depends on three important factors: the ball's **elasticity,** its temperature, and its internal friction.

Elasticity

Elasticity refers to a ball's "squeeze-ability" and how well it can return to its original shape after it hits something. Think about a ball of cookie dough, which is very "squeeze-able." If you dropped the ball of cookie dough on the floor, you would hear it plop. It would not bounce back to you because cookie dough is not elastic. In fact, a ball of cookie dough has such low elasticity that it would never regain its original shape.

A basketball, on the other hand, is not very "squeeze-able." When it bounces off the floor, it temporarily loses its shape, but this happens so quickly that it is normally not visible to the human eye. Then the ball regains its shape and springs back off the floor. The basketball returns to its original shape quickly because of its high elasticity. The best bouncing balls are those with the greatest elasticity.

Temperature

The outside temperature also affects a ball's bounce. Any tennis player will tell you that a ball bounces differently on a cold day than on a hot day. Why does this happen? The answer has to do with the movement of air molecules inside the ball.

Inside a hollow sports ball, molecules of air move at different speeds, depending on the ball's temperature. When the ball is warm, the air molecules move faster than when the ball is cool. As the air molecules move quickly inside the warm ball, they create more pressure which pushes out against the ball's cover. This pressure stretches the ball's cover and makes it less "squeeze-able." A warm ball has greater elasticity than a cooler one. This means that when the warm ball bounces, it regains its shape more quickly than a cooler ball.

A simple experiment can show how temperature affects a ball's bounce. Take four identical tennis balls. Place one in a freezer for at least three hours. Place the second in the refrigerator for at least three hours. Keep the third tennis ball warm by blowing on it with a blow dryer for ten minutes. *(Using the blow dryer for a longer period of time could be dangerous. Limit the time to ten minutes.)* Finally, keep the fourth ball at room temperature.

Take all four tennis balls from their location and drop them from the same distance onto a smooth surface. What happens to each ball? Which ball has the best bounce? The warmer tennis ball should have the highest bounce. Because the air molecules inside of it are moving quickly and pressing on its cover, the warmest tennis ball should have the greatest elasticity. In fact, its cover should even feel tighter than the covers of the other tennis balls.

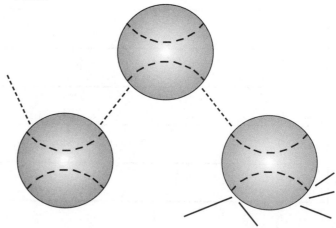

Internal Friction

If you rub the palms of your hands together very quickly, you feel heat. This heat is caused by **friction**, or rubbing one object against another. When you bounce a ball, the molecules inside bump into each other and produce friction, too. In the same way that you can create heat by rubbing your hands together, the molecules inside the ball also produce heat when they hit against each other.

What does this have to do with how well a ball will bounce? Some balls have a high degree of **internal** friction. When these balls bounce, the molecules inside bump into each other many times and produce a great deal of friction. This friction, in turn, makes a great deal of heat. Balls that produce so much heat energy cannot produce as much bouncing energy.

Some balls have a low degree of internal friction. When these balls bounce, the molecules inside them do not bump together as often and create little friction. As a result, they produce less heat energy than balls with a high degree of internal friction. Because they make less heat energy, they can make more bouncing energy.

Conclusion

A ball is a simple toy, but there is nothing simple about the science that affects its "bounce-ability." Learning about the factors that influence a ball's performance is interesting; it can also be useful. Some serious athletes might be able to make good use of information about a ball's elasticity and internal friction. What do you think?

Context Clues (I.B)
1. In this passage, the word **elasticity** refers to—

    A air molecules in a ball

    B how well a ball regains its shape

    C how high a ball can bounce

    D internal friction within a ball

Context Clues (I.B)
2. The word **friction** means—

    A air molecules bouncing against each other

    B the temperature inside a tennis ball

    C the bouncing energy of a ball

    D rubbing one object against another

Synonyms/Antonyms (I.D)
3. Which word is an ANTONYM for **internal**?

    A Farther

    B Elastic

    C Covered

    D Outer

Facts/Details (II.A)
4. According to the passage, balls with a high degree of internal friction—

    A bounce higher than other balls

    B have fewer air molecules inside them

    C produce a great deal of heat energy

    D produce a great deal of bouncing energy

Sequential Order (II.C)

5. In the experiment with tennis balls kept at different temperatures, what should you do before dropping the balls onto a smooth surface?

A Squeeze each one to tests its elasticity.

B Place all four balls in the freezer.

C Keep each of the four balls at different temperatures for a given period of time.

D Bump the balls together to check for internal friction.

Follow Directions (II.D)

6. According to the directions for the experiment, when you heat the tennis ball you should—

A limit the heating time to ten minutes

B place the ball on a smooth surface

C heat the ball for at least three hours

D check the ball's elasticity often when heating it

Paraphrase/Summarize (III.B)

7. Which of the following is the best summary of this passage?

A Balls with the greatest elasticity bounce the best.

B Balls with a low degree of internal friction produce very little heat.

C Several factors affect a ball's ability to bounce.

D Athletes need information about the factors that affect a ball's ability to bounce.

Cause/Effect (IV.A)

8. A ball kept in the freezer will not bounce as high as a ball kept at room temperature because the molecules in the colder ball—

A cause too much internal friction

B move quickly and make heat energy

C create too much pressure on the ball

D move slowly and reduce the ball's elasticity

Predictions (IV.B)

9. A ball with high elasticity and a low degree of internal friction would most likely—

A bounce very well

B not bounce at all

C bounce, but only once or twice

D bounce, but only on smooth surfaces

Inferences (V.A)

10. Knowing and applying information about the factors that affect a ball's ability to bounce could help a tennis player—

A win every competition

B spend less money by buying only the best tennis balls

C improve his/her playing ability

D become a more entertaining player

Interpretations/Conclusions (V.B)

11. According to information in this passage, which of the following combinations would most likely produce a ball with the highest bounce?

A High elasticity, low degree of internal friction, warm temperature

B Low elasticity, low degree of internal friction, warm temperature

C High elasticity, high degree of internal friction, cold temperature

D Low elasticity, high degree of internal friction, cold temperature

Author's Positions/Arguments (VI.D)

12. The author states that "there is nothing simple about the science that affects" a ball's ability to bounce to show that—

A simple toys do not reflect any scientific concepts

B science is too difficult for most people to understand

C a ball is a simple toy, but its bounce depends on several complex scientific principles

D people learn very little about science by studying how balls bounce

Fact/Opinion (VI.A)

13. Which of the following is an OPINION expressed in this passage?

A Air molecules move at different speeds, depending on the temperature.

B Friction occurs when one object rubs against another.

C Friction causes heat.

D Learning about the factors that influence a ball's performance is interesting.

Text Structure (II.B)

14. Imagine that your teacher asked you to read "Follow the Bouncing Ball" and take notes as you read. Write three facts and/or details on the note cards below. Make sure the information you list on each card relates to the topic listed on the card.

Card 1

> **Elasticity**

Card 2

> **Temperature**

Card 3

> **Internal Friction**

Response to Text (IV.D)

15. What advice would you give to a child who wants to buy a ball that has good "bounce-ability"? Use information from the text in your answer.

_____

_____

_____

_____

_____

_____

_____

_____

_____

_____

_____

_____

_____

_____

_____

_____

_____

10: How People Learned to Measure and Count

Throughout history, people have created useful tools for counting and measuring the items they use in their daily life. Even before they had a system for writing numbers, people developed methods to help them keep track of quantity, distance, and time. Many of these first counting and measurement tools may seem odd to us now, but they fulfilled a need long ago. In fact, some of these older tools led to our more modern methods of counting and measuring.

Fingers probably provided the first counting tools since they were "handy" and easy to use. Of course, since people only have ten fingers, they were limited in their counting. The first substitutes for fingers may have been small stones and sticks. As people counted their sheep, for instance, they would set aside one stone or stick to represent each animal. Some Indian tribes solved their counting problems with small pieces of rope. They simply tied a knot in the rope for each item they were counting. Other groups showed quantities by cutting notches in wood or making marks on the ground. People in China invented the **abacus**, a tool that uses beads to calculate amounts. In China and some other parts of the world, people still use the abacus today.

Counting was only one mathematical challenge faced by people long ago. We now have rulers and yardsticks, but long ago people did not have such tools to measure lengths and heights. Body parts became the **standard** method for determining various distances and lengths. The hand, for example, provided a **convenient** tool for measuring height. In fact, today we still measure a horse's height in "hands." People also used the human foot to measure lengths of cloth or pieces of land. Instead of purchasing a yard of material, a person bought material that was two foot-lengths (or two feet) long. Some of our modern measurement terms indicate the role that body parts once played in measurement systems.

Keeping track of time posed another challenge. Today, we depend on wrist watches and digital clocks, but at one time there were no watches or clocks as we know them. In place of today's clocks, candles offered one way to measure the passage of time. Marked off in sections, a candle clock took one hour to burn from one mark to the next one. Water clocks provided another method for telling time. Like the candle clock, the water clock had marked sections. As water drained from the clock and the water level dropped, these marks became visible and indicated how much time had **elapsed**. The hourglass was another popular timepiece used in the past. The sand in one end of the hourglass took an hour to fall to the other end. You probably don't use an hourglass today, but you may have its relative, the egg timer, in your kitchen.

It would be easy to poke fun at these old-fashioned methods of measurement and counting, but each one is an excellent example of creative thinking in action. Even without modern knowledge or equipment, people developed useful measurement tools that made their lives easier.

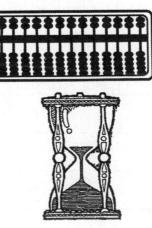

Context Clues (I.B)

1. The word **abacus** refers to—

   A a method for measuring length

   B a kind of clock

   C a counting device

   D small stones and sticks

Synonyms/Antonyms (I.D)

2. Which word is a SYNONYM for **elapsed**?

   A Presented

   B Parted

   C Passed

   D Provided

Multiple-Meaning Words (I.C)

3. In this passage, the word **standard** means—

   A flag or banner

   B required moral conduct

   C required

   D normal

Structural Cues (I.A)

4. The word **convenient** probably comes from the Latin word—

   A *conversari*, meaning "to associate with"

   B *convenire*, meaning "to be suitable"

   C *conventere*, meaning "to turn around"

   D *conventus*, meaning "assembly"

Facts/Details (II.A)

5. According to the passage, which of the following was used for counting?

   A Candles

   B Sand

   C Hourglasses

   D Stones and sticks

Paraphrase/Summarize (III.B)

6. Which of the following is the best summary of this passage?

   A People have always had trouble in counting and measuring.

   B Throughout history, people have developed ways to count and measure.

   C Counting and measurement tools of the past seem odd to people today

   D The human body provided the best measurement tools for people long ago.

Cause/Effect (IV.A)

7. Long ago people used their hands and feet for measuring length because—

   A they did not have measurement tools to use

   B they did not know how to use yardsticks

   C hands and feet provided the most accurate measurements

   D hands and feet were easier to use than other measuring tools

Inferences (V.A)

8. People no longer use water clocks or candle clocks because these clocks are—

A difficult to operate

B difficult to fix when they break

C not as accurate as clocks we have today

D too large for most homes

Interpretations/Conclusions (V.B)

9. After reading this passage, it seems clear that the measurement devices from long ago were—

A too difficult to use

B poor solutions for measurement problems

C creative methods for measuring and counting

D better than the measurement tools we have today

Author's Purpose (VI.B)

10. The author probably wrote this passage to—

A convince readers that older measurement tools were useless

B show that people who lived long ago were more creative than people today

C compare and contrast measurement tools of today with those of long ago

D explain some of the ways that measurement and counting problems were solved long ago

Bias/Propaganda (VI.E)

11. The author states that old methods of measurement and counting are "an excellent example of creative thinking in action." She says this because she wants readers to recognize that these methods—

A did not provide accurate measurements

B were better tools than modern ones

C demonstrated good problem-solving ability

D should be used today

Fact/Opinion (VI.A)

12. Which of the following is an OPINION expressed in this passage?

A Today we still measure a horse's height in "hands."

B An abacus is a tool that uses beads to count amounts.

C People once used fingers, stones, and sticks for counting.

D It would be easy to poke fun at old-fashioned methods of measurement and counting.

Figurative Language (VII.D)

13. The passage states that people developed methods to "keep track" of quantity, distance, and time. The phrase *keep track* means—

A invent new methods

B measure and count

C record and remember

D hunt for

82

Figurative Language (VII.D)

14. Write a paragraph that explains how the following sentence from the passage is a
play on words: Fingers probably provided the first counting tools since they were "handy"
and easy to use.

Response to Text (IV.D)

15. Write a composition that explains why modern clocks and watches would be considered more convenient than items like candle clocks and water clocks. Use information from the text in your answer.

_____

_____

_____

_____

_____

_____

_____

_____

_____

_____

_____

_____

_____

_____

_____

11: What kind of shopper are you?

Are you normally pleased with a purchase after you take it home? Sometimes a purchase doesn't live up to its advertising. Some problems are **minor**; for example, you may purchase the wrong size or color of clothing. You can easily correct this kind of problem. Most stores let customers return or exchange an incorrect item.

A purchase may displease you for a more serious reason. This kind of problem can be more difficult and frustrating to resolve. For example, a product may not fulfill the promises made in advertisements. Another product may require replacement long before you would expect. Most stores and companies are happy to help customers solve such problems, but sometimes a company will not cooperate with a dissatisfied buyer. Has this ever happened to you or your family? If so, then you may already know how difficult it can be to **resolve** the disagreement.

Consumers can avoid problems if they take some important steps before and after they purchase something. Each step involves some work and time, but smart consumers know that their efforts will be worthwhile.

Before You Buy

You should take several steps before you purchase a product so you can avoid trouble at a later time. First, think about what you want to buy. Which product or service features are most important to you? Sometimes shoppers do not begin with a clear idea of what they want. This kind of shopper must make too many important decisions during shopping time. Knowing what you need and want before you begin allows you to concentrate on getting the best deal once you are in a store.

Compare brands. Ask friends or family members who already have similar products to recommend the best brands. Magazines and newspapers often publish product comparison reports. Such reports usually discuss the features, price, and quality of similar products produced by different companies. Read these reports before you buy anything.

Compare stores. Not all stores offer the same quality, service, and bargains. Find a store that has a good reputation. It is usually easier to deal with this type of establishment. Plan ahead so you can take advantage of special sales. Store clerks can often tell you when a store will offer a certain product at a lower price.

Check for any extra charges—delivery fees, installation charges, service costs. Such costs vary from store to store and can add several dollars to a bill, erasing any bargain a store might give you.

Read the **warranty**, or written guarantee, for every product you want to buy. You should understand your responsibilities if you have a problem with a product after buying it. You should also understand the manufacturer's responsibilities for repair or replacement of a **defective** item.

Read all contract **terms** carefully. If you don't understand something, ask for an explanation. Make sure all blank spaces are completed before you sign a contract. If you have any doubts, show the contract to a legal expert before signing it.

Ask the sales person to explain the store's return or exchange policy before you purchase any product. Stores sometimes limit the time you have to return an item, while other stores require a receipt for any item that a customer wants to exchange or return.

Do not assume an item is a bargain just because a store says that it is. Compare prices at several stores so you will know when something is truly a bargain.

After You Buy

A smart consumer's job is not finished after a purchase. To avoid any problems, you should follow some guidelines after buying a product, too.

Always read and follow the instructions for using a product. Many times people think they know exactly how to operate or use an item, but not all products are the same. Many stores and companies will not exchange or take back an item if a customer does not follow the directions exactly.

Use a product only for its intended purpose. Again, most stores and companies will not accept an item for exchange or return if you have used it incorrectly. More importantly, using an item incorrectly can be dangerous.

Once you take a purchase home, reread the warranty. Remember that you may have more warranty rights in your state, since every state has its own laws for consumer protection.

Keep all sales receipts, warranties, and instructions in a safe place. You never know when you will need them.

If you have trouble with a product, report the problem to the company as soon as possible. Do not try to fix the product yourself because this may cancel the warranty altogether.

Keep a file of your efforts to solve any product problem. Your file should include the names of individuals you speak with, and the date, time, and outcome of each conversation. Keep copies of all correspondence, including letters you send to a company as well as the replies you receive.

Most purchases you make during your lifetime will probably meet your expectations. Like most consumers, though, you probably will encounter problems with some products. There is no way to prevent this from happening. If you know your rights and responsibilities, however, you can become a smarter consumer.

Source: U.S. Office of Consumer Affairs

Synonyms/Antonyms (I.D)
1. Which word is an ANTONYM for **minor** as it is used in this passage?

    A Adult

    B Secondary

    C Advertised

    D Significant

Context Clues (I.B)
2. The word **resolve** means—

    A argue

    B review

    C settle

    D fulfill

Context Clues (I.B)
3. The word **warranty** refers to—

    A product directions

    B a written guarantee

    C charges for delivery

    D a magazine advertisement

Multiple-Meaning Words (I.C)

4. In this passage, the word **terms** means—

A periods of time

B relationships among people

C words with certain meanings

D conditions of an agreement

Structural Cues (I.A)

5. The word **defective** probably comes from the Latin word—

A *defendere*, meaning "to ward off"

B *deferre*, meaning "to carry away"

C *defectus*, meaning "failure"

D *definire*, meaning "to limit"

Sequential Order (II.C)

6. What is the first step you should take before buying a product?

A Compare all brands of the product.

B Compare prices at several stores.

C Think about the features that are important to you.

D Read all contracts carefully.

Follow Directions (II.D)

7. What should you do if you do not understand a contract?

A Ask for an explanation.

B Make sure you complete all blank spaces on the contract.

C Sign the contract and show it to a legal expert.

D Read the warranty to find the answers.

Paraphrase/Summarize (III.B)

8. Which is the best summary for this passage?

A Comparing brands and stores are two ways to avoid problems when you purchase something.

B Consumers can avoid most problems when they purchase something if they follow important steps.

C Most people have problems when they go shopping.

D Most shopping problems are caused by stores and advertisements.

Cause/Effect (IV.A)

9. Some shoppers must make too many decisions during shopping time because they—

A compare too many brands

B shop at too many stores

C read contracts and warranties carefully

D do not know exactly what they need or want

Predictions (IV.B)

10. If a shopper follows the advice in this passage, the shopper is most likely to—

A have problems with products

B buy fewer items

C make better decisions about products

D shop at fewer stores

Interpretations/Conclusions (V.B)

11. You should keep a file of your efforts to solve a product problem because—

   A companies will not answer your letters

   B companies will not help consumers who don't have files

   C this makes it easier to recall steps you've taken to solve the problem

   D this is the best way to avoid buying something you don't want

Generalizations (V.C)

12. From information in this passage, a reader could reasonably conclude that most companies are—

   A dishonest in advertisements

   B cooperative with consumers

   C careless with products

   D unconcerned about customers

Recognize Author's Appeals

13. The author encourages readers to be better shoppers by—

   A focusing on a company's responsibility to please customers

   B presenting examples of what happens when people do not shop wisely

   C telling about a personal experience when the author was not pleased with a purchase

   D providing specific steps a person should follow before and after buying a product

Author's Positions/Arguments (VI.D)

14. The author of this passage seems to believe that—

   A consumers have little control over their purchases

   B most stores are unwilling to help dissatisfied customers

   C consumers always need legal advice when they complain to a company

   D consumers can often avoid problems when shopping

Fact/Opinion (VI.A)

15. Which is an OPINION expressed in this passage?

   A Magazines and newspapers often publish product comparison reports.

   B Not all stores offer the same quality, service, and bargains.

   C Most stores and companies are happy to help customers solve problems.

   D Stores sometimes limit the time a consumer has to return a product.

Paraphrase/Summarize (III.B)

16. Imagine that your teacher asked you to summarize "What kind of shopper are you?" for your classmates. Write a one- to two-paragraph summary that you might present.

12: The Elephant That Will Not Move

This passage by Arthur Brisbane was originally published in various Hearst newspapers throughout the United States.

In the zoo of New York, a poor elephant has stood in chains for years. The animal was thought to be **vicious**, and was kept fastened tightly to one spot, that it might have no chance to do damage.

A short time ago its keeper became convinced that the elephant would do no harm and might safely be unchained. The chains were taken off, and the keeper thought with satisfaction that the poor beast would now enjoy freedom and be made happy by the possibility of moving freely about its large **enclosure**.

The elephant did not move. The chains were gone, it was no longer tied, but it stood, and it still stands, in just the same spot.

The habit of slavery had become too strong. The elephant, though free, stands still, sadly swaying its heavy head, **ignorant** of the freedom that has come to it.

Men and women and children who see the elephant, and other men who write paragraphs for the newspapers, **dilate** on the poor animal's "stupidity."

"The elephant has been called the most intelligent of animals," says one writer, "but this elephant, that doesn't know when the chains are off, seems to prove that the elephant can be a good deal of a fool."

How easy it is for us to see the faults in others, our fellows, and the animals below us. But which one of us can truly say that he is not in exactly the same position as that poor elephant, fixed to one spot by the chains of long ago?

Are we not still standing as a race just as we stood years and centuries ago, ignorant of the freedom that has come to us? Thousands of splendid men have worked, lived, and died to free us from superstition and ignorance, yet still we stand in the same place, and fail to appreciate the freedom that is ours. Millions of us, tied down by foolish superstition, are like that elephant—the chains are off, but we stand still.

The road to peace, happiness, and progress has been shown to us in the teachings of great leaders, but we still stand in the same old place, fighting, hating, cheating, suspecting, and harming one another. Here and there is a little progress. Gradually we begin to appreciate and enjoy the freedom that has been given to us with the striking away of old mental chains. The progress is slow.

Look into your own mind. Do you take advantage of all the possibilities that are before you? Do you use your brain to control your existence, acts, and habits for your own benefit and the benefit of others? If not, you ought to sympathize with this poor elephant.

Context Clues (I.B)
1. The word **vicious** means—

   A satisfied

   B damaged

   C savage

   D confined

Synonyms/Antonyms (I.D)
2. Which word is a SYNONYM for **enclosure** as it is used in this passage?

   A Gate

   B Cage

   C Freedom

   D Container

Structural Cues (I.A)
3. The word **ignorant** probably comes from the Latin word—

   A *idea*, meaning "idea"

   B *plicare*, meaning "to fold"

   C *importare*, meaning "to carry in"

   D *ignorare*, meaning "not to know"

Multiple-Meaning Words (I.C)
4. In this passage, the word **dilate** means—

   A act

   B widen

   C write

   D open

Main Idea (III.A)
5. This passage is mostly about—

   A why elephants must be chained

   B why elephants should not be chained

   C the similarities between elephants and people

   D people's inability to recognize and enjoy freedom

Cause/Effect (IV.A)
6. The elephant did not move after being unchained because it did not—

   A know it was free

   B care about its freedom

   C trust people

   D have great intelligence

Inferences (V.A)
7. According to the author of this passage, people make slow progress because they—

   A have had poor leadership

   B do not have many freedoms

   C do not appreciate their freedoms

   D enjoy life the way it is

Interpretations/Conclusions (V.B)
8. The author tells the story about the elephant to—

   A explain why elephants should be freed

   B justify keeping elephants in zoos

   C prove that people behave in foolish ways

   D teach something about human behavior

Interpretations/Conclusions (V.B)
9. Which of the following would support the author's view that people have made little progress?

   A New medical discoveries allow people to live longer lives.

   B Red Cross workers help in countries where natural disasters have occurred.

   C People of different races and religious beliefs wage war against each other.

   D World leaders work together to solve disagreements among different countries.

Generalizations (V.C)

10. Which word would the author most likely use to describe people's use and appreciation of their freedoms?

   A Adequate

   B Limited

   C Ideal

   D Foolish

Recognize Author's Appeal

11. To support his stand, the author of this passage does NOT include—

   A his personal opinion

   B figurative language

   C comparison

   D specific examples of people's behavior

Author's Positions/Arguments (VI.D)

12. The author of this passage seems to believe that people—

   A cannot change their ways

   B do not want freedom

   C allow old beliefs to limit their progress

   D appreciate the freedom they have

Author's Positions/Arguments (VI.D)

13. Which word would the author most likely use to describe the human race's progress?

   A Impressive

   B Disappointing

   C Complete

   D Frightening

Identify Genres (VII.A)

14. This passage would be best described as—

   A an article

   B an editorial

   C a short story

   D a biographical sketch

Literary Elements (VII.C)

15. The author uses the elephant as a—

   A simile

   B personification

   C symbol

   D figure of speech

Main Idea (III.A); Response to Text (IV.D)

16. Write a brief composition that addresses the following questions: What is the author's main message in this passage? Do you agree or disagree with the author's main message? Why or why not?

13: Into the Primitive

In the late 1800s, gold was discovered in Alaska, and hundreds of men joined the Klondike Gold Rush in search of fortune. The following passage is adapted from the first chapter of Jack London's Call of the Wild, *which tells of one dog's experience in the rush for Alaskan gold.*

Buck did not read the newspapers, or he would have known that trouble was brewing for him and every other strong, muscular dog on the west coast. Faraway in the cold arctic darkness, men had found a yellow metal, and thousands more men were rushing into the Northland. These men wanted heavy dogs, with strong muscles for work and furry coats to protect them from the frost.

Buck lived at Judge Miller's place, a big house in the Santa Clara Valley. A wide, cool verandah ran around the four sides of the house. Gravel driveways wound through wide lawns and under the boughs of tall poplars. At the rear, things were even more **spacious** than at the front. There were great stables, where a dozen grooms and boys worked. There were rows of servants' cottages, an endless and orderly array of out-houses, long grape arbors, green pastures, orchards, and berry patches. Then there was the pumping plant for the artesian well, and the big cement tank where Judge Miller's boys took their morning **plunge** and kept cool in the hot afternoon.

Over this great estate Buck ruled. Here he was born and here he had lived the four years of his life. It was true, there were other dogs, but they did not count. They came and went, resided in the crowded kennels, or lived in the recesses of the house like Toots, the Japanese pug, or Ysabel, the Mexican hairless—strange creatures that rarely put nose out of doors or set foot to ground.

Buck was neither house-dog nor kennel-dog. The whole **realm** was his. He plunged into the swimming tank or went hunting with the Judge's sons. He escorted Mollie and Alice, the Judge's daughters, on long twilight or early morning rambles. On wintry nights, he lay at the Judge's feet before the roaring library fire. He carried the Judge's grandsons on his back, or rolled them in the grass, and guarded their footsteps through wild adventures down to the fountain in the stable yard and beyond. Among the other dogs, he stalked **imperiously**, and Toots and Ysabel he utterly ignored. He was king—king over all the creeping, crawling, flying things of Judge Miller's place, humans included.

His father, Elmo, a huge St. Bernard, had been the Judge's companion, and Buck did fair to follow in the way of his father. He was not so large—he weighed only one hundred and forty pounds—for his mother, Shep, had been a Scotch shepherd dog. Nevertheless, one hundred and forty pounds, along with the dignity that comes of good living and respect, enabled him to carry himself in royal **fashion**. During the four years since his puppyhood, he had lived the life of an **aristocrat**. He had a fine pride in himself, but saved himself by not becoming a pampered house-dog. Hunting and other outdoor delights had kept down the fat and hardened his muscles.

So this was the manner of Buck in the fall of 1897, when the Klondike strike dragged men from all the world into the frozen North. But Buck did not read the newspapers, and he did not know that Manuel, one of the gardener's helpers, was an undesirable **acquaintance**. Manuel had one serious failing—he loved to gamble. And to gamble, he needed money.

The Judge was at a meeting, and the boys were busy organizing a club, on the night of Manuel's **treachery**. No one saw him and Buck go off through the orchard on what Buck thought was a stroll. Except for one man, no one saw them arrive at the little station known as College Park. This man talked to Manuel, and money clinked between them.

"You might wrap up the goods before you deliver them," the stranger said gruffly. Manuel doubled a piece of rope around Buck's neck under the collar.

Buck accepted the rope. He had learned to trust in the men he knew, and to give them credit for a wisdom greater than his own. But when the ends of the rope were placed in the stranger's hands, Buck growled. To his surprise, the rope tightened, shutting off his breath. In a quick rage, he sprang at the man, who grabbed Buck by the throat and threw him on his back. Then the rope tightened even more. Never in all his life had Buck been treated so cruelly, and never in his life had he been so angry. But his strength weakened, and he knew nothing when the train stopped and the two men threw him into the baggage car.

Synonyms/Antonyms (I.D)
1. Which word is a SYNONYM for **spacious**?

   A Narrow

   B Bright

   C Noisy

   D Roomy

Multiple-Meaning Words (I.C)
2. In this passage, the word **plunge** means—

   A fall

   B swim

   C adventure

   D toss

Context Clues (I.B)
3. The word **realm** means—

   A situation

   B pasture

   C population

   D kingdom

Multiple-Meaning Words (I.C)
4. In this passage, the word **fashion** means—

   A form

   B kind

   C style

   D influence

Structural Cues (I.A)

5. The word **imperiously**, which means "lordly" or "proudly," probably comes from the Latin word—

   A *plantare*, meaning "to plant"

   B *pendere*, meaning "to hand"

   C *impingere*, meaning "to pus"

   D *imperare*, meaning "to command"

Context Clues (I.B)

6. Which of the following would be considered an **aristocrat**?

   A Servant

   B Relative

   C Professor

   D Princess

Context Clues (I.B)

7. An **acquaintance** is someone that you—

   A have known for many years

   B consider part of your family

   C know only slightly

   D call your best friend

Synonyms/Antonyms (I.D)

8. Which word is an ANTONYM for **treachery**?

   A Confidence

   B Loyalty

   C Freedom

   D Friendship

Sequential Order (II.C)

9. Buck growls at the stranger—

   A as soon as he sees the man

   B after Manuel places the rope in the man's hands

   C after the man throws Buck on his back

   D before Manuel puts the rope around Buck's throat

Cause/Effect (IV.A)

10. According to the passage, Buck does not know trouble is "brewing" because he—

   A gets along well with Judge Miller's family

   B does not read the newspaper

   C knows how to protect himself

   D does not spend time with the other dogs

Predictions (IV.B)

11. Which of the following will most likely happen in the next part of the story?

   A Manuel will rescue Buck and take him back to Judge Miller.

   B The stranger will return Buck to Judge Miller.

   C Buck will be taken far away to work in the cold arctic.

   D Manuel will win money by gambling and buy Buck from the stranger.

Inferences (V.A)

12. Manuel sells Buck to the stranger because he—

A knows Buck will work hard for the stranger

B knows Buck is fierce and dangerous

C needs money for gambling

D believes Judge Miller is unkind to Buck

Interpretations/Conclusions (V.B)

13. Judge Miller and his family probably treat Buck differently than the other dogs because they—

A know he is a royal dog

B think of him as a pet

C are afraid of him

D know Manuel is going to sell him

Generalizations (V.C)

14. Which word best describes Buck's life before Manuel sells him to the stranger?

A Uncertain

B Miserable

C Risky

D Comfortable

Identify Genre (VII.A)

15. This passage is taken from—

A an autobiography

B an essay

C a novel

D a myth

Genre Characteristics (VII.B)

16. This passage would be considered fiction because it includes—

A background information about the Klondike Gold Rush

B a setting that places the story in both a specific place and time period

C a description of Judge Miller's estate

D an explanation of a dog's life in the cold arctic weather

Literary Elements (VII.C)

17. The major conflict in this passage takes place between—

A Buck and Judge Miller

B Judge Miller and Manuel

C Manuel and the stranger

D Buck and the stranger

Literary Elements (VII.C)

18. Manuel meets the stranger—

A at Judge Miller's place

B at the kennels

C at a railway station

D in the Klondike

Figurative Language (VII.D)

19. In the passage, it states that Buck did not know "trouble was brewing." This means that Buck did not know—

A how to protect himself from Manuel and the stranger

B Judge Miller planned to get rid of him

C he might be taken from his home

D he would have to live in a kennel

20. List at least three elements of fiction found in "Into the Primitive" and explain how each one is represented in the passage.

Element of Fiction	Represented in "Into the Primitive"

Study Skills

VIII. Identify and use sources of different types of information

A. Use and interpret graphic sources of information
B. Use reference resources and the parts of a book to locate information
C. Recognize and use dictionary skills

Practice 1: Study Skills

Directions: Read each question. Then choose the best answer. On your answer sheet, darken the circle for the correct answer.

1. To locate the copyright date for a book, you would normally look—

   A in the index

   B on the cover

   C in the table of contents

   D on the page directly after the title page

2. To locate the name of the company that published a book, you would normally look—

   A in the index

   B on the title page

   C in the table of contents

   D in the glossary

3. Toby wants to know how many major units are in his social studies book. He should look—

   A on the cover

   B in the foreward

   C on the title page

   D in the table of contents

4. A brief summary of a book's content often appears—

   A on the back cover

   B in the index

   C on dedication page

   D with the acknowledgements

5. Gloria wants to review the characteristics of mammals before taking her science test. To find the exact page where she can locate this information, she should look—

   A in the glossary

   B on the cover

   C in the index

   D in the preface

6. To find the names of people who helped an author write a book, you would normally read the—

   A preface

   B table of contents

   C acknowledgements

   D title page

7. An author's explanation of a book's purpose is usually found—

   A in the index

   B in the glossary

   C in the preface

   D on the dedication page

8. Which of the following would be included in a book's bibliography?

   A the book's copyright date

   B definitions of terms used in the book

   C references used by the author

   D a list of people who assisted the author in writing the book

Practice 2: Study Skills

Directions: Read each question. Then choose the best answer. On your answer sheet, darken the circle for the correct answer.

To answer the questions, use information on these labels from three household cleaning products.

Clean-Air Disinfectant Spray

Warning: Avoid contact with eyes and food.

Physical Hazards: Flammable. Contents under pressure. Do not use near fire, sparks, or flame. Exposure to temperatures above 130°F may cause bursting. Do not use on polished wood, leather, rayon fabrics, or acrylic plastics.

Storage/Disposal: Store in original container. Keep away from children. When product container is empty, replace cap and discard in trash. Do not puncture or burn. Do not reuse empty container.

Active Ingredients: O-Phenylphenol 1.1%, Ethanol 79%.

Jiffy Multi-Purpose Cleaner

Warning: Hazardous to humans and domestic animals.

Caution: May cause eye irritation. Avoid contact with eyes.

First Aid: If sprayed or splashed in eyes, immediately remove contact lenses and rinse eyes with plenty of water for at least 15 minutes.

Storage/Disposal: Store out of reach of children. Refill container only with Jiffy Multi-Purpose Cleaner. If not refilling, rinse empty container thoroughly and discard in trash or recycle.

Fresh-Ease Room Spray

Warning: Can cause skin or severe eye irritation. Avoid breathing spray mist.

First Aid: Eyes—Immediately flush eyes with plenty of water. Skin—Wash skin with soap or mild detergent. Apply skin cream. Seek medical attention if irritation results. Inhaling—Move person to fresh air at once. Get medical attention if breathing does not return to normal.

Storage/Disposal: Keep out of reach of children. Keep container closed and stored in a dry area at temperatures between 40°F and 120°F.

For emergency medical assistance, call your local poison control center.

---

1. According to the labels, all three products—
   A have contents under pressure
   B have reusable containers
   C should be kept away from children
   D cannot be used on wood

2. Based on the information on their labels, all three products are—
   A effective
   B safe for the environment
   C hazardous
   D expensive

3. When empty, the container for Clean-Air Disinfectant Spray should be—
   A refilled
   B discarded
   C stored in a cool area
   D rinsed out

4. According to the labels, all three products can damage—
   A wooden furniture
   B empty containers
   C a person's skin
   D a person's eyes

5. Which information is NOT included on all three labels?
   A a warning
   B storage and disposal directions
   C ingredients
   D product name

Practice 3: Study Skills

Directions: Read each question. Then choose the best answer. On your answer sheet, darken the circle for the correct answer.

The following product descriptions appeared in a computer catalog. Use the information to answer the questions.

High-quality Advantage diskettes. Available in basic black or rainbow colors. You can rely on these high-density diskettes, guaranteed to last a lifetime. Shipped in convenient plastic storage box.		
Item #	**Description**	**Price**
39140	3.5HD 30 pk color w/$15 mail-in rebate	$5.99
39141	3.5HD 30 pk black w/$15 mail-in rebate	$4.99
39138	3.5HD 50 pk color w/$20 mail-in rebate	$9.99
39137	3.5HD 50 pk black w/$20 mail-in rebate	$8.99
39129	3.5HD 100 pk color w/$30 mail-in rebate	$19.99
39127	3.5HD 100 pk black w/$30 mail-in rebate	$17.99

Advanz-Age Computers are the fastest, most reliable computers on the market! You don't have time for anything else! Scan our prices—you won't find such powerful computers at a lower price. Our powerful new models meet the demands of the fast-paced workplace. They come loaded with software for word processing, graphics, spreadsheets, games... and more! Have instant access to the Internet with the 56K modem included in every model. And, of course, every model comes with the Advanz-Age 24/7 Technical Supportline—our support staff is available 24 hours a day, 7 days a week to help you analyze and solve technical problems over the phone!

Item #	Model	Processor/ Speed	Hard Drive	RAM	CD-ROM	Regular Price	Sale Price
45281	ADZ300	300MHz	3.0GB	64MB	24X	$949	$899
45282	ADZ333P	333MHz	3.0GB	64MB	24X	$1,099	$950
45283	ADZ333M	333MHz	3.2GB	64MB	24X	$1,249	$1,179
45284	ADZ400	400MHz	4.1GB	128MB	24X	$1,499	$1,299
45285	ADZ400P	400MHz	5.0GB	128MB	32X	$1,649	$1,529
45286	ADZ400M	400MHz	6.1GB	128MB	32X	$1,729	$1,599
45287	ADZ450	450MHz	6.1GB	128MB	32X	$1,849	$1,729
45288	ADZ450P	450MHz	8.0GB	256MB	32X	$1,999	$1,849

1. What is the LEAST you could pay for a computer with a 32X CD-ROM?

   A $1,729

   B $1,649

   C $1,529

   D $1,499

2. If you wanted a computer with a 400MHz processor and 24X CD-ROM, which model would you buy?

   A ADZ300

   B ADZ400

   C ADZ400P

   D ADZ450

3. Which of the following is NOT included in any of the Advanz-Age Computers?

   A 56K modem

   B software

   C scanner

   D hard drive

4. How much RAM is included in Model ADZ400M?

   A 400MHz

   B 6.1GB

   C 128MB

   D 32X

5. If you need 150 black diskettes, you should order items—

   A 39141 and 39137

   B 39137 and 39127

   C 39138 and 39127

   D 39129 and 39138

6. From information included in the descriptions, you could conclude that—

   A the Advanz-Age computers with the slowest processor speeds cost the most

   B all computers come with a 56K modem

   C computers with a 24X CD-ROM must have at least a 4.0GB hard drive

   D Advanz-Age computers with the fastest processors and the largest hard drives cost more than others

7. Which of the following is a FACT expressed in the catalog descriptions?

   A Advanz-Age Computers are the fastest, most reliable computers on the market.

   B Advantage diskettes are shipped in plastic storage boxes.

   C Advanz-Age Computers meet the demands of the fast-paced workplace.

   D You can trust Advantage diskettes.

8. The only Advanz-Age computer with a 3.2GB hard drive is model—

   A ADZ400M

   B ADZ400

   C ADZ333M

   D ADZ200P

9. Which Advanz-Age computer regularly costs $1,729?

   A Model ADZ450

   B Model ADZ400P

   C Model ADZ333M

   D Model ADZ400M

Practice 4: Study Skills

Directions: Read each question. Then choose the best answer. On your answer sheet, darken the circle for the correct answer.

The following charts include general information about the 1964 Winter and Summer Olympic Games and the final medal standings for the top ten countries that competed. Use the information in the charts to answer the questions.

1964 Winter Olympic Games

Location: Innsbruck, Austria
Dates: January 29–February 9, 1964
Number of nations that competed: 36
Total number of competitors: 1,093
Number of women: 200

Nation	Gold	Silver	Bronze
USSR	11	8	6
Austria	4	5	3
Norway	3	6	6
Finland	3	4	3
France	3	4	—
Sweden	3	3	1
Germany	3	2	3
United States	1	2	4
Canada	1	1	1
Netherlands	1	1	—

1964 Summer Olympic Games

Location: Tokyo, Japan
Dates: October 10–24, 1964
Number of nations that competed: 93
Total number of competitors: 5,140
Number of women: 683

Nation	Gold	Silver	Bronze
United States	36	26	28
USSR	30	31	35
Japan	16	5	8
Germany	10	22	18
Italy	10	10	7
Hungary	10	7	5
Poland	7	6	10
Australia	6	2	10
Czechoslovakia	5	6	3
Great Britain	4	12	2

1. Based on information in the charts, you can conclude that—

   A few athletes from the United States competed in the 1964 Winter Olympic Games

   B the USSR had the greatest number of athletes competing in the 1964 Winter Olympic Games

   C Czechoslovakia did not compete in the 1964 Winter Olympic Games

   D Norway won more medals in the 1964 Winter Olympic Games than Austria

2. Based on information in the charts, you can conclude that—

   A the USSR had the best overall performance in both the Winter and Summer Olympic Games of 1964

   B France did not compete in the 1964 Summer Olympic Games

   C more countries participated in the 1964 Winter Olympic Games than in the 1964 Summer Olympic Games

   D people in the United States do not enjoy the sports played in the Winter Olympic Games

3. Which group of nations were top-ten medal winners in both the Winter and Summer Olympic Games of 1964?

   A USSR, Austria, and Poland

   B USSR, United States, and Japan

   C USSR, Germany, and United States

   D USSR, Austria, and Norway

4. Of the nations listed in the chart, which won the fewest number of medals in the 1964 Summer Olympic Games?

   A Netherlands

   B Great Britain

   C Canada

   D Czechoslovakia

5. How many nations competed in the 1964 Winter Olympics?

   A 10

   B 36

   C 93

   D 200

6. The 1964 Summer Olympic Games were held in—

   A Innsbruck, Austria

   B the USSR

   C the United States

   D Tokyo, Japan

7. In the 1964 Winter Olympic Games, the United States performed—

   A better than any other nation

   B worse than any other nation

   C better than Canada and the Netherlands

   D better than in the 1964 Summer Olympic Games

Practice 5: Study Skills

Directions: Read each question. Then choose the best answer. On your answer sheet, darken the circle for the correct answer.

The Rodriguez family is planning a trip to Canada. At the library, Mrs. Rodriguez used the computer card catalog to find resources with information about that country. Details from title cards for the books appear below. Use the information from the cards to answer the questions.

917.10464	
Title	Baedeker Canada
Other Title	Canada
Publisher	New York, New York: Macmillan Travel, ©1996
Description	color illustrations; color maps
Series Title	Baedeker Travel Guides
Notes	Translated from German Text: Bernard Abend, et al 2nd ed. Country map (color; folded to 18 cm) inserted in jacket
Subject(s)	Canada Guidebooks
Other Entries	Abend, Bernard
Format	Serial

917.10464	
Title	Canada/Garry Marchant; photography by Ken Straiton
Author	Marchant, Garry
Publisher	Oakland, CA: Compass American Guides, ©1991
Description	308 p.: color illustrations
Series Title	Discover Canada
Subject(s)	Canada description and travel, 1981–Guidebooks Canada description and travel, 1981–Views

Video 917.10464	
Title	Discovering Canada/ International Video Network
Publisher	San Ramon, CA: International Video Network, ©1992
Description	1 videocassette (73 min); color
Series Title	Video Visits, Canadian Collection
Notes	VHS format Title on box: Canada
Subject(s)	Canada, description and travel
Other Entries	International Video Network

Video 917.10464	
Title	Canada/GLL TV Enterprises, Inc.
Publisher	Plymouth, MN: Simitar Entertainment, ©1991
Description	1 videocassette (90 min); color
Series Title	Passport Travel Guide Journey to Adventure
Notes	Videocassette release of the film by GLL TV Enterprises, Inc. VHS format
Performer/ Narrator	Gunther Less
Summary	Host Gunther Less explores Montreal, Toronto, Quebec City, Alberta, and Saskatchewan
Subject(s)	Videocassettes Travel video recordings Canada, description and travel
Other Entries	Less, Gunther L. GLL TV Enterprises Simitar Entertainment, Inc.

917.1	
Title	Canada, Provinces and Territories/ Lynda Sorenson
Author	Sorenson, Lynda
Publisher	Vero Beach, FL: Rourke Book Co., ©1995
Description	24 p.: color illustrations, map
Series Title	Exploring Canada
Notes	Includes index
Subject(s)	Canada Canada, political divisions Canada, territories and possessions
Format	Juvenile

1. What company publishes the Passport Travel Guide series?

   A Compass American Guides

   B Rourke Book Co.

   C Simitar Entertainment

   D GLL TV Enterprises, Inc.

2. *Canada* by Garry Marchant was published in—

   A 1981

   B 1991

   C 1992

   D 1995

3. Mrs. Rodriguez will probably find the most recent travel information about Canada in—

   A the book titled *Canada, Provinces and Territories*

   B the video recording titled *Discovering Canada*

   C the book titled *Canada*, by Garry Marchant

   D the travel guide titled *Baedeker Canada*

4. *Canada, Provinces and Territories* does not include—

   A color illustrations

   B an index

   C a fold-out map

   D any maps

5. *Discovering Canada* was created in—

   A 1973

   B 1981

   C 1991

   D 1992

6. To find other books about the provinces of Canada, Mrs. Rodriguez could look under the following category:

   A videocassettes

   B Canada, political divisions

   C Rourke Book Co.

   D Bernard Abend

7. *Discovering Canada* is part of a series titled—

   A International Videos

   B Discover Canada

   C Video Visits

   D Exploring Canada

8. The video recording by Simitar Entertainment is the only listed resource that has—

   A information about Canadian provinces

   B a narrator

   C color illustrations

   D a country map

9. *Baedeker Canada* was—

   A first published in German

   B written by Gunther Less

   C published in Canada

   D included in the Passport Travel Guide series

Practice 6: Study Skills

Directions: Read each question. Then choose the best answer. On your answer sheet, darken the circle for the correct answer.

The following film schedule appeared in the entertainment section of the newspaper.

The Plaza Cinema	
2367 W. Plaza Drive	555-333–4444

Two-day Advance Tickets at Box Office Regular Price: $6.00	
Credit Cards Accepted *$3.00 Bargain Matinees • No Passes	Stadium Seating Tuesday Discount All Day + No Bargain Matinees

Once Upon a Time	*11:00 *12:45 *2:55 5:40 8:35
Yesterday Is Gone	*11:25 *1:40 3:55 6:00 9:55
Double Trouble	*11:40 *12:55 3:45 5:55 8:40
Home in Rome	*12:00 *2:55 4:10 6:30 8:15
The Party	*12:15 *1:55 3:10 5:10 9:10
The Lion's Roar •	*12:00 3:00 6:00 9:00
The Little Soldier •+	1:15 4:05 7:30
The War •+	12:10 2:05 5:40 9:15

1. According to the film schedule, bargain matinees—

   A occur only on Tuesdays

   B cost $4.00

   C do not accept passes

   D occur before 3:00 each day

2. If Eric gets off work at 9:15 and arrives at the theater by 9:30, he would be able to see—

   A *Once Upon a Time*

   B *Yesterday Is Gone*

   C *The War*

   D *The Party*

3. Janet wants to see two films. If she sees the 12:00 showing of *Home in Rome* and it ends at 2:15, which is the first film she could see from its beginning?

   A *Yesterday Is Gone*

   B *The Lion's Roar*

   C *Once Upon a Time*

   D *The War*

4. Mr. Franco arrived at the theater at 3:35. Which is the first film he could see?

   A *Yesterday Is Gone*

   B *Double Trouble*

   C *The Party*

   D *The Little Soldier*

5. Based on information in the film schedule, which of the following statements is accurate?

   A On Tuesday, you can see *The War* for $3.00.

   B *The Little Soldier* is the least popular film being shown at The Plaza Cinema.

   C You need a special pass to see *The Lion's Roar*.

   D There is only one bargain matinee for *The Lion's Roar*.

6. Jerry and Tim can meet to see a movie any time between 5:00 and 6:30. They will NOT be able to see—

   A *The Little Soldier*

   B *The Party*

   C *Yesterday Is Gone*

   D *Double Trouble*

108

Practice 7: Study Skills

Directions: Read each question. Then choose the best answer. On your answer sheet, darken the circle for the correct answer.

To find the information you need in reference books, you must know where and how to find it.

1. If you used an encyclopedia to find information about the climate of northern Canada, under which key term would you look?

   A climate

   B storms

   C Canada

   D North America

2. To find the word **factory** in a dictionary, you would look on a page with the following guide words:

   A fabric–face

   B face–fact

   C fact–factual

   D factual–fading

3. Which information about a word is usually NOT included in a dictionary?

   A pronunciation

   B rhyming words

   C origin

   D other forms of the word

4. Which shows the correct pronunciation for the word **naughty**?

   A nô′ tē

   B nō′ tē

   C nô   tē′

   D no′ tī′

5. If you used an encyclopedia to find information about the human nervous system, under which key term would you look?

   A human beings

   B human body

   C psychology

   D systems

6. Which word would NOT be found on a dictionary page with **examine** and **exchange** as guide words?

   A example

   B excerpt

   C exchange

   D excite

7. If you used an almanac to find out how much oil the United States imported in 1995, under which key term would you probably look?

   A awards

   B vital statistics

   C public opinion

   D energy

8. If you used an encyclopedia to find specific information about the art and music of ancient Greek civilization, under which key term would you look?

   A ancients

   B art and music

   C civilization

   D Greece

Practice 8: Study Skills

Directions: Read each question. Then choose the best answer. On your answer sheet, darken the circle for the correct answer.

Which resource would be best for finding each of the following?

1. An antonym for the word **predictable**
   A an almanac
   B an encyclopedia
   C a thesaurus
   D an atlas

2. The population of the USA in 1990
   A an atlas
   B an almanac
   C an encyclopedia
   D a dictionary

3. The size of Spain in square miles
   A an almanac
   B a globe
   C a dictionary
   D a map

4. The states that border Ohio
   A a dictionary
   B an almanac
   C an encyclopedia
   D an altas

5. An article about the recent discovery of remains from an ancient civilization
   A *Business Week*
   B *Reader's Digest*
   C *National Geographic*
   D *Field and Stream*

6. Comparison of different brands of washing machines
   A *Business Week*
   B *Home and Garden*
   C *Consumer Reports*
   D *Popular Mechanics*

7. A report on the recent World Peace Conference held in Paris
   A *Newsweek*
   B *National Geographic*
   C *People*
   D *Business Week*

8. The wedding of your favorite movie star
   A *Reader's Digest*
   B *Newsweek*
   C *Business Week*
   D *People*

9. A preview of the coming professional basketball season
   A *Newsweek*
   B *Sports Illustrated*
   C *Reader's Digest*
   D *Field and Stream*

10. Decorating ideas for kitchens and dining rooms
    A *Field and Stream*
    B *People*
    C *Consumer Reports*
    D *Home and Garden*

Practice 9: Study Skills

Directions: Read each question. Then choose the best answer. On your answer sheet, darken the circle for the correct answer.

The chart shows the final record for several teams in the local teen basketball league.

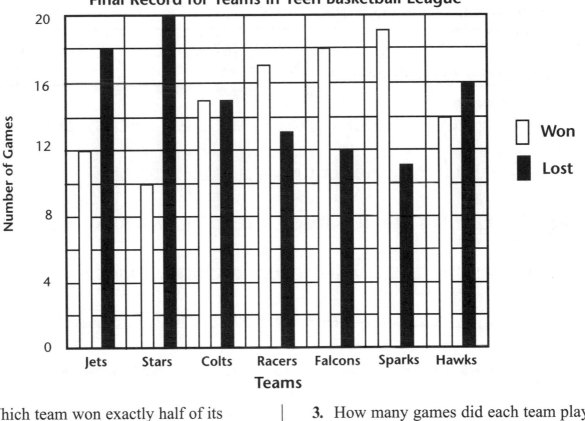

Final Record for Teams in Teen Basketball League

1. Which team won exactly half of its games?
   - **A** Jets
   - **B** Stars
   - **C** Colts
   - **D** Racers

2. Which team won half as many games as it lost?
   - **A** Sparks
   - **B** Colts
   - **C** Falcons
   - **D** Stars

3. How many games did each team play?
   - **A** 20
   - **B** 25
   - **C** 30
   - **D** 35

4. Which two teams had opposite records?
   - **A** Jets and Hawks
   - **B** Stars and Sparks
   - **C** Racers and Falcons
   - **D** Jets and Falcons

Practice 10: Study Skills

Directions: Read each question. Then choose the best answer. On your answer sheet, darken the circle for the correct answer.

Marci likes to use the Internet to find information for her school assignments. The diagram shows the home page for a Web site that she found. Use it to answer the following questions.

Welcome to YourInfo.net!
Today is Thursday, January 6

Easy shopping
Gifts under $10

The Music Store
Today's hits for less

World News | *THE FRONT PAGE* *PEOPLE AND PLACES* *MONEY & TRADE* *EDITORIALS* *NEWS QUIZ*

National News | *THE FRONT PAGE* *PEOPLE AND PLACES* *STOCK NEWS* *EDITORIALS*

Local News | *THE FRONT PAGE* *PEOPLE AND PLACES* *PLACES TO GO–THINGS TO DO* *TRAFFIC*

Entertainment | *STAR UPDATE* *AT THE MOVIES* *TV & RADIO* *GOOD BOOKS* *MUSIC NOTES*
PUZZLES & GAMES

Weather | *TODAY'S WEATHER MAP* *THE WEEK AHEAD* *AROUND THE WORLD* *WEATHER TRIVIA*

Sports | *THE NBA* *THE NFL* *PLAYER PROFILES* *COLLEGE SPORTS* *LOCAL SPORTS NEWS* *FUN FACTS*
SPORTS CROSSWORD

The Health Center | *NUTRITION AND DIET* *FITNESS FOR YOU* *TALK TO THE DOCTOR*
THE COLD & FLU SEASON *HEALTH QUIZ*

The Research Place | *ENCYCLOPEDIA* *DICTIONARY* *THESAURUS* *THE HISTORY PLACE*
THE SCIENCE PLACE *THE WRITING CENTER* *ALMANAC* *ATLAS*

Travel | *THE TRAVEL AGENT* *TRAVEL BARGAINS* *MAPS AND TRAVEL GUIDES* *SUMMER DESTINATIONS*

Can't find it? Search the Web ...

[   ]
Enter key word/words

[**Search**]

Today's Quote

"Act as if what you do makes a difference. It does." —William James

Today's Top Stories

President Says US Will Help Poor Nations

Storms in Europe Disrupt Travel

Firefighters Save Ten Children in Boston

Doctors Say Cure for Cancer Is Possible

Coldest Air of Season to Arrive on Saturday

NBA's Top Two Teams Fight for Top Spot

---

1. What is the name of this Web site?

   A The Music Store

   B Search the Web

   C YourInfo.net

   D Today's Top Stories

2. Where will Marci and her friends find a a review of the movie *Tag, You're It*?

   A Money & Trade

   B At The Movies

   C Today's Quote

   D Editorials

3. In a report on the economy, Marci realizes she uses the word business too often. For another word, she'd click—

   A Thesaurus

   B The Writing Center

   C Fitness for You

   D Traffic

4. Marci's cousin from England is coming to visit. Where would Marci look to find information about discounted airfare?

   A Star Update

   B Good Books

   C Summer Destinations

   D Travel Bargains

5. Where would Marci look to find the daily calorie needs of children?

   A The Travel Agent

   B Nutrition and Diet

   C Atlas

   D Today's Top Stories

6. Mike, Marci's older brother, claims he scored the winning shot in last night's basketball game against Richardson High. Where could Marci find out if he did?

   A Sports Crossword

   B Local Sports News

   C Fun Facts

   D Weather Trivia

7. Where would Marci look to help her cousin Sally pack the right clothes for her visit?

   A Travel Bargains

   B Traffic

   C Good Books

   D The Week Ahead

8. Marci's math class follows the stock market. She wants to know if her stock in Bozos-R-Us, a clown-supply company, has risen since yesterday. She'd check—

   A Money and Trade

   B Today's Quote

   C People and Places

   D The History Place

9. Marci and her friends have a holiday from school and want to attend an art festival. To find the price of tickets, they'd check—

   A Travel Bargains

   B Stock News

   C Talk to the Doctor

   D Places to Go—Things to Do

Practice 11: Study Skills

Directions: Study the map of Canada. Then read each question and choose the best answer. On your answer sheet, darken the circle for the correct answer.

1. In which Canadian province is Lake Winnipeg located?

   A Winnipeg

   B Northwest Territories

   C Ontario

   D Manitoba

2. Which Canadian province does NOT border on Hudson Bay?

   A Manitoba

   B Quebec

   C British Columbia

   D Ontario

3. The national capital of Canada is—

   A Montreal

   B Ontario

   C Ottawa

   D Churchill

4. Which of the following statements is true?

   A Denmark is the northernmost province in Canada.

   B The Labrador Sea is northeast of Quebec.

   C The national capital of Canada is in British Columbia.

   D Canada shares a border with Russia.

5. What is the approximate distance between Edmonton and Winnipeg?

   A 500 miles

   B 750 miles

   C 1500 miles

   D 2000 miles

6. Of the cities shown on the map, which appears to be the southernmost city in Canada?

   A Vancouver

   B Regina

   C Toronto

   D Halifax

7. Which lake does NOT form part of Ontario's border?

   A Lake Huron

   B Lake Erie

   C Lake Ontario

   D Lake Michigan

8. Which city is northwest of Edmonton?

   A Whitehorse

   B Calgary

   C Victoria

   D Saskatoon

9. In which Canadian province is Great Slave Lake located?

   A Northwest Territories

   B Saskatchewan

   C Yukon Territory

   D New Brunswick

10. Which city is approximately 500 kilometers from Calgary?

    A Victoria

    B Saskatoon

    C Edmonton

    D Regina

Practice 12: Study Skills

Directions: Look at the map which shows part of Indianapolis, Indiana. Read each question and choose the best answer. On your answer sheet, darken the circle for the correct answer.

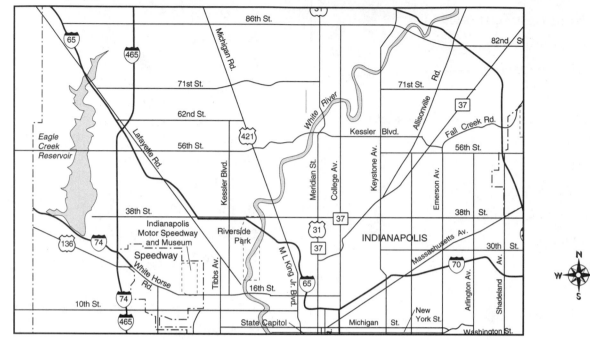

1. The State Capitol is located—

   A southwest of the Motor Speedway

   B north of 71st Street

   C east of Arlington Avenue

   D southeast of Riverside Park

2. On this map, Michigan Road/Highway 421 does NOT cross—

   A 56th Street

   B 71st Street

   C Meridian Street

   D 38th Street

3. According to this map, numbered streets in Indianapolis run—

   A northeast to southwest

   B northwest to southeast

   C north and south

   D east and west

4. To reach Michigan Road from her home on 86th Street west of Highway 465, Tanya normally travels south on Highway 465, then east on 71st Street. If a traffic accident blocks traffic on 71st Street, what other street or road could Tanya take to reach Michigan Road?

   A Highway 74

   B Kessler Blvd.

   C Keystone Av.

   D 62nd St.

5. Which two highways share the same route through part of Indianapolis?

   A Highway 421 and Highway 31

   B Highway 70 and Highway 465

   C Highway 465 and Highway 74

   D Highway 136 and Highway 65

Scoring Guidelines for Open-Ended Questions

Connect/Compare/Contrast

An effective response will include:
- a clear introduction that identifies the issues, characters, etc., to be connected, compared, and/or contrasted
- a clear, effective organizational plan to handle connections, similarities, and/or differences
- specific details that clearly identify connections, similarities, and/or differences
- clear transitions from one part of the response to another
- a clear, logical conclusion that summarizes the points made in the response

Use these scoring guidelines with the following open-ended questions—

"Two Poems," p. 45, #10
"Along Came a Spider," p. 55, #17
"A Tree from the Past," p. 72, #20a*

This question does not require a written composition as a response. To evaluate responses, focus on the student's selection/use of specific details and correct placement within the Venn diagram.

Genre Identification/Characteristics
Literary Elements/Figurative Language

When identifying the correct genre of a reading selection or the literary elements included in a selection, students should mention several of the following characteristics—

Fiction
- use of the basic elements (character, setting, problem, solution)
- sequence of events leading to a resolution (plot)
- purpose: to entertain

Nonfiction
- emphasis on factual events/information
- purpose: to explain, argue, persuade

Poetry
- use of stanza/verse form
- focus on sound devices (e.g., rhyme, alliteration, onomatopoeia)
- use of figurative language (e.g., similes, metaphors)

Use these scoring guidelines with the following open-ended questions—

"Two Poems," p. 46, #11
"Athena and Arachne," p. 51, #17*
"The Wind in a Frolic," pp. 65-66, #12 and #13
"How People Learned to Measure and Count," p. 83, #14
"Into the Primitive," p. 98, #20*

This question does not require a written composition as a response. To evaluate responses, focus on the student's selection of specific examples to depict the literary element(s) addressed in the question.

Main Idea and Paraphrase/Summarize

An effective response will include:
- a clear focus on the text's major ideas
- omission of extraneous details/information
- a clear, accurate statement of the text's basic message/content

Use these scoring guidelines with the following open-ended questions—

"It's a Noisy World Out There!" p. 41, #18
"A Simple Way to Save Lives," p. 60, #18
"A Tree from the Past," p. 73, #20b
"What kind of shopper are you?" p. 89, #16
"The Elephant That Will Not Move," p. 93, #16

Response to Text

An effective response will include:
- a clear focus on important ideas presented in the text
- a response that connects the text's major ideas to the writer's personal experiences and prior knowledge
- questions, speculations, or observations that relate logically and clearly to the text
- clear, logical elaboration of ideas with relevant information from both the text and the writer's experiences
- clear transitions from one part of the response to another
- a clear, logical conclusion that summarizes writer's response to the text

Use these scoring guidelines with the following open-ended questions—

"Do you know how to make recycled paper?"
    p. 36, #19
"It's a Noisy World Out There!" p. 42, #19
"Athena and Arachne," p. 51, #17*
"Along Came a Spider," p. 55, #17
"A Simple Way to Save Lives," p. 61, #19
"A Tree from the Past," p. 72, #20a*
"Follow the Bouncing Ball," p. 79, #15
"How People Learned to Measure and Count,"
    p. 84, #15
"The Elephant That Will Not Move," p. 93, #16

*This question does not require a written composition as a response. To evaluate responses, focus on the student's selection/use of specific details and correct placement within the Venn diagram.

Text Structure

An effective response will include:
- information pertinent to the given passage
- obvious use of text structure to locate and organize information from the text
- evidence that a coherent paragraph or composition could be written with the information provided

Use these scoring guidelines with the following open-ended questions—

"Follow the Bouncing Ball," p. 78, #14*

*This question does not require a written composition as a response. To evaluate responses, focus on the student's selection and organization of information from the text.

Scoring Rubrics for Open-Ended Questions

In most states that administer tests with open-ended questions requiring student-written responses, evaluators use scoring rubrics to assess these responses. A scoring rubric is an assessment tool designed to determine the degree to which a writer meets the established criteria for a given writing task.

Many scoring rubrics allow for holistic evaluation, which focuses on the overall effectiveness of the written response rather than individual errors in content, organization, mechanics, etc. For example, a scoring rubric might allow a teacher to score papers on a scale from 1 (for the least effective responses) to 4 (for the most effective responses). Rubrics that offer a broader scale of points (e.g., 1–6) allow for a more refined evaluation of a written response. For example, with these rubrics it is possible for evaluators to distinguish between an outstanding response (e.g., 6) and a very good response (e.g., 5). Rubrics with a narrow scale of points (e.g., 0–2) do not allow for a very refined evaluation, generally limiting evaluators to a response of either "pass" or "fail."

Sample scoring rubrics appear on the following pages. They offer several options for evaluating the written responses students complete for the open-ended questions in *TestSMART®*. A brief description of each rubric follows.

Note: Teachers may also use scoring rubrics provided for their own state's competency test.

Three-point rubric: This rubric has a narrow scale of points and, therefore, limits the scoring to basically pass–fail. The three-point rubric is most appropriate for brief written responses (2-4 sentences). In addition, this rubric works well with the short answers recorded on graphic organizers (e.g., Venn diagrams).

Four-point rubric: This rubric provides a wider scale of points, making a more refined evaluation possible. It does not, however, allow teachers to make clear distinctions between outstanding responses and those that are merely good. The four-point rubric is appropriate for brief written responses (2-4 sentences) and longer responses (two or more paragraphs).

Six-point rubric: Because of the broad scale of points, this rubric allows for a more refined evaluation of a written response. The six-point rubric is appropriate for longer responses (two or more paragraphs).

Three-Point Rubric

2
Provides complete, appropriate response
Shows a thorough understanding
Exhibits logical reasoning/conclusions
Presents an accurate and complete response

1
Provides a partly inappropriate response
Includes flawed reasoning/incorrect conclusions
Overlooks part of question/task
Presents an incomplete response
Shows incomplete understanding

0
Indicates no understanding of reading selection
Fails to respond to question/task

Four-Point Rubric

4
Focus on topic throughout response
Thorough, complete ideas/information
Clear organization throughout
Logical reasoning/conclusions
Thorough understanding of reading task
Accurate, complete response

3
Focus on topic throughout most of response
Many relevant ideas/pieces of information
Clear organization throughout most of response
Minor problems in logical reasoning/conclusions
General understanding of reading task
Generally accurate and complete response

2
Minimal focus on topic/task
Minimally relevant ideas/information
Obvious gaps in organization
Obvious problems in logical reasoning/conclusions
Minimal understanding of reading task
Inaccuracies/incomplete response

1
Little or no focus on topic/task
Irrelevant ideas/information
No coherent organization
Major problems in logical reasoning/conclusions
Little or no understanding of reading task
Generally inaccurate/incomplete response

Six-Point Rubric

6
Full focus on topic throughout response
Thorough, complete ideas/information
Clear, maintained organizational pattern throughout
Clearly logical reasoning/conclusions
Thorough understanding of reading task
Accurate, complete response

5
Focus on topic throughout most of response
Very thorough ideas/information
Clear organization throughout majority of response
Generally logical reasoning/conclusions
Overall understanding of reading task
Generally accurate and complete response

4
Focus on topic/task but with obvious minor digressions
Sufficient relevant ideas/information
Minor gaps in organization in parts of response
Minor problems in logical reasoning/conclusions
Above average understanding of reading task
Minor inaccuracies that affect quality and thoroughness of response

3
Focus on topic/task but with obvious major digressions
Relevant ideas/information mixed with irrelevant material
Major gaps in organization
Somewhat logical reasoning/conclusions
Basic understanding of reading task
Several inaccuracies that affect quality and thoroughness of response

2
Little or no focus on topic/task throughout response
Few relevant ideas/pieces of information included in response
Lack of organizational plan
Illogical reasoning/conclusions throughout response
Lack of basic understanding of reading task
Generally inaccurate/incomplete response

1
Unacceptable response due to severe problems in focus, relevancy, organization, and/or logical reasoning/conclusions
No understanding of reading task

Vocabulary List

abacus	bisect	data	eliminate	fidget
abbreviate	bizarre	deciduous	embed	finance
abnormal	blemish	decline	embrace	financial
abode	boggle	decoy	emotion	flair
absolute	bothersome	deduct	emotional	flexible
acceptance	brawl	defective	encircle	flinch
accumulate	candid	defiant	enclosure	flora
accusation	canister	deflate	endanger	floral
acquaintance	capering	defy	endeavor	flourish
admirable	cashier	delegate	endless	forceful
admittance	casual	delegation	endure	forerunner
ado	cavity	dental	enlarge	foretell
adversity	certify	depart	enrage	forlorn
advisable	chide	depicting	enrich	former
afloat	chronicle	deprive	enshrine	fortify
aggressive	chronology	despise	entangle	foul
alight	civilian	detain	entrap	fowl
align	clarity	devise	entrust	fragrant
allot	clasps	devote	envious	friction
ally	clause	devotion	envision	frill
alter	clearance	dictate	epoch	frolic
ambitious	clerical	dilate	era	frustrate
ample	comparable	dimension	erupt	futuristic
analyze	compartment	dire	eternal	gadget
angular	compete	discarded	etiquette	gape
annoyance	compromise	discharge	evacuate	garble
antiseptic	condense	discord	evident	gross
appliance	confer	discount	exceed	grudge
applicant	confidence	dislocate	excess	halting
appraise	confidential	dislodge	exclude	hardy
apprehensive	confine	disown	exert	harsh
apt	conquest	dispatch	exile	heir
aristocrat	consequence	displease	expectation	heiress
assumption	constrain	disrespect	expelled	hilarious
assurance	contend	distinctive	expertise	humane
astride	convenience	distribute	exposure	hygiene
attentive	convenient	docile	exquisite	identical
available	cordial	domestic	extends	identify
aviator	corrective	donor	extract	identity
barricade	crag	doubtless	extrovert	idle
bay	cringe	duplicate	factor	ignite
beacon	criteria	efficient	falter	ignorant
begrudge	crucial	elaborate	fashion	immense
bewilder	crumple	elapsed	fateful	impair
bicker	cunning	elasticity	faulty	imperfect
billow	currency	elation	favorable	imperiously
biological	custody	elegant	ferocious	impose

impress	lofty	oversight	requirement	survival
imprint	logic	paradox	resolve	survivor
improper	logical	pare	respectable	suspension
impulse	lope	passion	retain	suspicion
inability	lunge	pastime	ridicule	symbolic
inadequate	lyrics	peddle	rile	symbolize
incapable	madcap	penalty	rouse	tempo
incomplete	maneuver	percentage	rowdy	tendency
indefinite	mangle	perish	sane	term
inefficient	mantle	persist	scandal	territorial
infect	margin	plea	scoff	textile
infinite	marshy	plunge	securely	texture
inflame	maximum	pollutant	security	theft
inflate	meddle	pose	segment	tinge
inflection	membranes	postpone	selective	toil
informal	menacing	predate	seminar	token
ingest	merit	preferable	sensitive	tolerate
inquiry	mingle	premium	sentiment	trait
inspire	minor	preoccupied	separation	transform
instill	minority	privilege	sequence	transformed
instinct	minute	probable	shatter	transmit
interact	misplace	process	shimmering	transplant
internal	modify	procession	shortage	treachery
interruption	monarch	profile	shrine	trundled
intramural	motivation	propel	shrivel	uncertainty
intravenous	motive	proverb	significance	uninhibited
intricate	multiple	puncture	slander	unpredictable
introvert	muscular	pursue	slight	uphold
intrude	mystify	quake	smirk	usable
invalid	myth	racial	socialize	utmost
invasion	nigh	racket	solitary	vacancy
isolate	nominate	rallying	spacious	vend
issue	nourish	random	sparse	vent
itemize	numerous	realm	specialize	ventilate
jargon	oath	reap	specialty	vial
jest	obstruction	recent	specify	vicious
justify	occupant	recovery	spiderlings	warranty
juvenile	occur	refer	spite	welfare
kernel	omit	refined	squad	woe
kindle	option	reflex	stammer	wretched
lair	optional	reform	standard	yearn
latter	orchestrate	refresh	stationary	
lessen	ornamental	relapse	stationery	
linear	outpace	rematch	submerge	
linger	overcome	remote	supine	
literary	overlap	renewal	supportive	
locale	overrule	reproduce	surplus	

Name _____   Date _____

Comprehension: Passage # _____   Vocabulary: Practice # _____

Study Skills: Practice # _____

Answer Sheet

1. Ⓐ Ⓑ Ⓒ Ⓓ   15. Ⓐ Ⓑ Ⓒ Ⓓ

2. Ⓐ Ⓑ Ⓒ Ⓓ   16. Ⓐ Ⓑ Ⓒ Ⓓ

3. Ⓐ Ⓑ Ⓒ Ⓓ   17. Ⓐ Ⓑ Ⓒ Ⓓ

4. Ⓐ Ⓑ Ⓒ Ⓓ   18. Ⓐ Ⓑ Ⓒ Ⓓ

5. Ⓐ Ⓑ Ⓒ Ⓓ   19. Ⓐ Ⓑ Ⓒ Ⓓ

6. Ⓐ Ⓑ Ⓒ Ⓓ   20. Ⓐ Ⓑ Ⓒ Ⓓ

7. Ⓐ Ⓑ Ⓒ Ⓓ   21. Ⓐ Ⓑ Ⓒ Ⓓ

8. Ⓐ Ⓑ Ⓒ Ⓓ   22. Ⓐ Ⓑ Ⓒ Ⓓ

9. Ⓐ Ⓑ Ⓒ Ⓓ   23. Ⓐ Ⓑ Ⓒ Ⓓ

10. Ⓐ Ⓑ Ⓒ Ⓓ   24. Ⓐ Ⓑ Ⓒ Ⓓ

11. Ⓐ Ⓑ Ⓒ Ⓓ   25. Ⓐ Ⓑ Ⓒ Ⓓ

12. Ⓐ Ⓑ Ⓒ Ⓓ   26. Ⓐ Ⓑ Ⓒ Ⓓ

13. Ⓐ Ⓑ Ⓒ Ⓓ   27. Ⓐ Ⓑ Ⓒ Ⓓ

14. Ⓐ Ⓑ Ⓒ Ⓓ   28. Ⓐ Ⓑ Ⓒ Ⓓ